THE
COLETTE GUIDE
TO SEWING KNITS

PROFESSIONAL TECHNIQUES
FOR BEAUTIFUL EVERYDAY GARMENTS

BY ALYSON CLAIR

Text copyright © by Alyson Clair
Photographs © by Colette Patterns

First published in The United States by Colette Patterns, a division of Colette Media, Portland, OR.

ISBN 978-0-615-99916-6

www.colettepatterns.com
www.alysonclair.com

Design by Sheli Ben-Ner
Photography by Sarai Mitnick
Editing by Sarai Mitnick
Technical illustration by Kristen Blackmore

First Edition, 2014

THE MONETA DRESS,
DESIGNED BY ALYSON CLAIR
FOR COLETTE PATTERNS

Pattern available at
colettepatterns.com
and at independent retailers

INTRODUCTION

When most people learn to sew, they start with woven fabrics. Because wovens are what we're comfortable with, I've noticed a knowledge gap on the subject of working with knit fabrics at home.

I'm here to assure you that if I can learn to sew with knits, anyone can.

I did not learn to sew until the age of 22. Though I have a degree in apparel design, most of my knowledge about knits comes from trial and error on the job in the apparel industry where I've worked as a patternmaker and technical designer for the last eight years. Today, I'm a senior apparel developer in the activewear industry in addition to running my own knitwear line, Clair Vintage Inspired. A willingness to play with fabric and try new things will take you far when it comes to sewing knits; it did for me.

Today, 97% of the apparel sold in the United States is made outside of the country. With most of the workforce and machinery overseas, it's no wonder so much knowledge has been lost. I want to bridge that gap, and make you as excited about knits as I am.

This book is divided into 3 parts. We'll start by talking about materials in Part 1, including fabric, needles, thread, and trims.

Part 2 covers machines. I understand that not everyone has a serger or coverstitch machine. The first portion of this section is focused on using a serger, as that is the most common way to sew stretch fabrics for durability and movement. But there are other methods of sewing knits, and we'll cover those alternatives as well. If you find yourself excited by knits, a serger may be something you invest in later, and the serger methods will still come in handy for you.

Finally, in Part 3 we'll go over techniques, including laying, cutting, fitting, seaming, and finishing. I always try to create garments that could hang on a rack with anything that was sewn anywhere else in the world, both in terms of quality and construction, and this section will show you how.

Knits can be an entirely new game, but it's the only one I want to play. I hope you enjoy creating with knits as much as I do.

PART 1

MATERIALS

CHAPTER 1

FABRIC

What do you think of when you imagine fabric shopping? And what do you see when you look in your fabric stash?

Even though I've been working with knits for a long time, cotton woven fabric is the first thing that comes to mind when I imagine visiting a fabric store. Woven fabrics, like the plentiful printed cottons you see, are typically stable and very easy to work with. It's the bread and butter of many fabric stores.

Now go to your closet and your dresser. Take a look at the textile selection in front of you. I bet it's rather different from your fabric stash. You probably have underwear, socks, t-shirts, sweaters, leggings, and dresses all made from knits. Not only that, but I bet the selection of knits is pretty diverse.

WHAT IS A KNIT?

Knit fabrics have a completely different structure from wovens because of the way they're manufactured. This greatly affects the mechanics of how the fabric behaves.

Woven fabrics are made by doing an over and under method on a loom at 90 degree angles. The warp is the yarn that is held in the loom, and the weft is the yarn that travels through the warps as the fabric is woven. If you have ever done any craft weaving it is essentially the same technique, just much smaller in scale.

This method of creating fabric is structurally sound, and unless the fabric has spandex in it, the only stretch you find in a simple woven is a slight amount in the wefts, or if you are using the fabric on the bias.

WOVENS

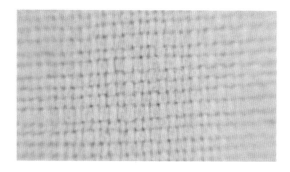
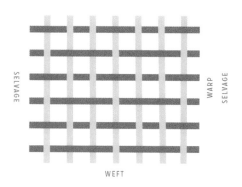

There are all sorts of variations of woven fabrics, including jacquards, brocades, twills, and more; they are all structured and designed to be stable fabrics.

KNITS

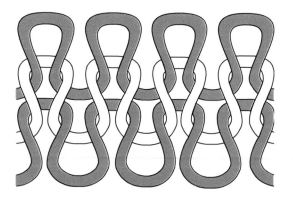

Knits are an entirely different animal. Their looped structure gives them a great deal of stretch.

HOW KNITS ARE MADE

Knit fabrics are created on a knitting machine, which is different from a weaving loom. The yarns are interlocked at a 45 degree angle to create a structure of loops. If you have ever hand knitted, this is the same method. The most common method to create fabrics is called **weft knitting**, which uses a single yarn.

Warp knitting is a method in which more than one yarn is used. This type of knitting can only be done by machine. Warp knitting produces very stable knits, like tricot. Most commonly it can be seen in women's shapewear and supportive lingerie, along with high performance athletic garments, like compression products.

Rib knits are fabrics that have alternating knit and purl stitches within the fabric. These fabrics have a lot of stretch and are commonly found in t-shirt collars, hoodie cuffs, and letterman jacket cuffs and collars. Rib knits can be created as pieces, where they are knit to specific widths for garments, or they can be produced as yardage. If you want a good example, take a look at the cuff of one of your sweaters.

Circular knits (also called tubular knits) are knits that are literally knit in a circle, similar to the way socks are knit on a circular knitting needle. A good example would be a basic men's t-shirt. Many are just knit tubes with no side seams. These tubes are cut into strips. The shoulders are then cut at an angle along with a curve for armholes. Circular knits can be used as is, slit open to create full width, or just treated like a piece of fabric that has been folded in half.

FIBERS

Knits can be made of nearly anything: cotton, polyester, rayon, silk, lurex, nylon, wool, and more! The content can also be mixed from any of the above, or have spandex added in.

One of the most interesting fabrics I've used for dresses was a wool/lurex/spandex blend. It was beautiful, but if I had checked the content first I most likely never would have touched it and fallen in love. After all, isn't all wool supposed to be itchy? That's why I always touch first when shopping and look at content second. Touching fabrics will give you an idea of how they will feel and drape on the body.

COTTON

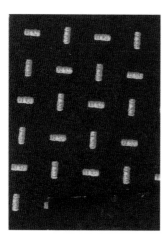

Cotton knits and cotton knit blends are great to sew with, although they can sometimes lack good recovery. Recovery refers to the ability of the fabric to return to its original shape after being stretched. Much depends on the weight, hand, stretch, and finish of the fabric. We'll discuss recovery and how to check for it when we discuss shopping for fabric (see p. 25).

PROS

- *Natural fiber*
- *Wears well*
- *Comfortable*
- *Easy to care for*

CONS

- *Often more rigid than other knits, which may not be optimal for items that require a lot of drape, such as dresses.*
- *Lightweight versions can be very sheer and not appropriate for full dresses or unlined tops*
- *100% cotton has minimal vertical stretch*
- *Often lacks stretch recovery*

POLYESTER

Polyester gets a bad rap because many people don't like the way it feels, or they prefer breathable natural fibers. But polyester can be a good choice sometimes, and it blends well with other fibers.

PROS

- *Wears well if cared for correctly and a quality fabric is used*
- *Lightweight versions are great for drapey garments*
- *Washes cold and line dries well without much extra need for pressing*
- *Polyester blends are stretchy and durable*

CONS:

- *Hand feel can be undesirable to some people.*
- *Less breathable than natural fibers*
- *Poor quality versions can pill quickly*
- *Difficult to remove stains*

SILK

Silk is a luxurious fiber, often with a sheen that gives it a distinctive look. Silk knits can make for some very slinky, drapey garments.

PROS

- Luxurious hand feel
- Strong and durable
- Insulates the body
- Comfortable to wear
- Takes dye well, so colors are often very saturated

CONS

- Can be expensive

RAYON

Rayon is not exactly natural or synthetic, but somewhat in between. It's a beautifully soft fiber that wears well. Modal is a type of rayon.

PROS:

- Soft hand feel
- Wears well
- Blends well with spandex or other materials
- Travels and steams well
- Cool to the touch and absorbent

CONS

- Shrinks if washed in warm water or machine dried

WOOL

Wool fibers are made from the fleece of sheep or other domestic animals. You likely have at least one wool sweater, in which case you are probably familiar with the warmth and strength of this fiber.

PROS

- Insulating
- Breathable
- Absorbent
- Can be very soft, with a luxurious hand feel

CONS

- Some varieties can be coarse or itchy

NYLON

Nylon is a synthetic fiber, often blended with other fibers to create durable fabrics with great recovery.

PROS

- Strong and durable
- Great deal of stretch
- Recovers well
- Keeps its shape over time
- Easy to care for

CONS

- Hand feel can be undesirable to some people.

ALL ABOUT STRETCH

Now that you have a basic idea of how knits and wovens differ and the kinds of fibers knits can be made from, let's talk about stretch. Think about your own wardrobe and how much stretch you have in it. Could you imagine a bra that didn't stretch? What about yoga pants, a sweater, underwear, or leggings? There are two things that make knit fabrics stretch: mechanical stretch and yarn stretch.

MECHANICAL STRETCH

The first kind of stretch comes from the actual structure of the knit and is called mechanical stretch. You see the majority of the stretch in the weft, or selvage to selvage, of the fabric.

Knit fabrics are created by interlocking loops of thread. When the fabric is pulled, the space in the middle of each loop allows the fabric to stretch. This is mechanical stretch.

This cotton knit stretches because the structure of the knit allows for it. The tiny loops of yarn are being expanded as the fabric is pulled.

YARN STRETCH

In addition to mechanical stretch, additional stretch may come from the actual yarns in the fabric. This is called yarn stretch. These yarns include stretch fibers such as spandex (also called by the brand name Lycra) or elastane. Yarn stretch works together with the mechanical stretch of the fabric. Most dressmaking knits have 3-8% spandex, but it's not uncommon to find up to 20% spandex in shapewear.

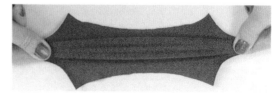

A knit fabric that has spandex content will have both mechanical stretch and yarn stretch.

When this fabric is pulled, the structure allows the fabric to stretch. At the same time, the threads themselves are also stretching because of the spandex content. Notice how much farther this fabric with spandex stretches than the cotton knit with only mechanical stretch.

HORIZONTAL STRETCH

Knit fabrics should stretch easily from selvage to selvage. We call this the horizontal stretch.

VERTICAL STRETCH

The stretch of a fabric parallel to the selvage is called the vertical stretch. Knit fabrics often have more horizontal than vertical stretch, and some have no vertical stretch at all.

CHOOSING YOUR STRETCH

The most important thing to consider when buying a knit is the end use and how you want the fabric to perform with the design. This is where the vertical and horizontal stretch comes into play. Here are some things to think about when choosing stretch fabrics.

If you are working with a snug fitting design that does not have much ease, look for a fabric that has both vertical and horizontal stretch. This dress is made from a 4-way stretch modal with spandex which has both mechanical stretch and yarn stretch.

If you are working on a loose garment that has more drape, then stretch is not as much of a consideration. For this dress, a cotton knit without spandex works fine.

HOW KNITS ARE LABELED

There are many terms to describe knits, which is why stores often organize them in different ways. Some are labeled by type, some by end use, and some aren't labeled at all. Here are common terms you will most likely encounter when shopping for knits and what they mean.

JERSEY

Typically, a jersey knit is a single yarn knit fabric. It can be made from anything, from a soft wool to the type of polyester that would be appropriate for a soccer uniform. It is typically drapey and has a pliable hand. It can be labeled a single jersey, double jersey, interlock jersey, or jacquard jersey, which are terms that refer to the type of knitting used to make the fabric. If you look closely, you can usually tell the right side from the wrong side, except for interlock jersey, which is thicker and looks similar on both sides.

SPANDEX

If you see this section, it indicates a selection of fabrics with some spandex content, not fabric made of 100% spandex. Not only would that be insanely expensive, it would feel like a giant rubber band! If you see a part of the store organized under this name you will most likely find a variety of fabrics like polyester, nylon, rayon, cotton, and anything else, all knit with around 4%-20% spandex.

RIBBED KNIT

This type of knit is usually found on t-shirt collars and sweater cuffs. If knit specifically for cuffs and collars, the rib feels strong and tight. These ribbed knits are usually not as wide as other knit fabrics and can be costly. You can also find lighter weight rib knits that are as wide as normal fabrics. Think about using light rib knits for tank tops, and tight ribbed knits for bands around the edges of other garments.

NYLON OR TRICOT

Nylon or tricot fabrics are used more often for slips, nightgowns, or underwear than for dresses or separates. The weights of these fabrics can range from almost sheer to opaque. Sometimes lingerie fabrics can be found in this area.

This is a picture of a vintage printed tricot, most likely intended for pajamas or loungewear.

LINGERIE

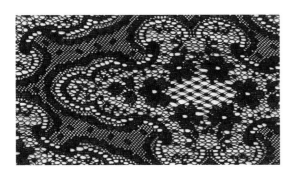

In this section, you may find the nylon or tricot mentioned above, along with powermesh, stretch lace, and all sorts of other fun fabrics, depending on how big the section is at your store. My favorite is 4 way stretch lace when it's available. Don't be afraid to experiment and use lingerie fabrics on non-lingerie garments such as skirts and dresses!

SWEATER KNITS

Sweater knits are typically a single yarn knit and can have a huge variety in content, thickness, and weight. You can absolutely use them for a sewing project! When shopping, check to see if the pattern is knit into the fabric, or if it is a solid fabric with the print over the top. Usually the printed sweater knits are knit with finer yarns and are more similar in look and feel to the other knit fabrics we've discussed.

FLEECE

You could find all sorts of things in this area, including traditional brushed back fleece for sweatshirts, French terry (shown here), and stretch polar-like fleeces. If you are looking for a heavy-weight fabric, I suggest French terry. It's easy to find a good quality fabric and it has a looped back side so it won't pill when washing.

STRETCH WOVENS VS. KNITS

When you are looking for knit fabrics, don't be tempted to substitute with a stretch woven. These are woven fabrics that typically have spandex in them and are sometimes lumped together with knits.

Don't get my wrong, I think they are great. Unfortunately, they do not perform the same because they lack the mechanical stretch that knits have (see p.16). If you use them on a knit project, you'll probably wind up with a garment that you can't get into once finished, so save them for a woven pattern when you know you're going to need a little extra stretch. If you are unsure if the fabric you are looking at is knit or woven look at the cut edge of the fabric for indication.

DOUBLE KNIT OR PONTE KNIT

Though double knits and ponte knits do not have the exact same knit structure, they are similar in weight and hand and are often labeled interchangeably. I usually select either of these when making a bottom, like the Colette Patterns Mabel skirt. They are dense, durable, stretchy, and most of all, provide modesty. These fabrics are great for showing off curves while also smoothing due to their thickness, eliminating VPL (visible panty lines). You can find fabrics that will stretch in all directions and that have a nice hand.

ITY

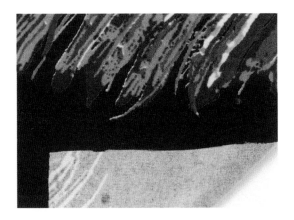

ITY is an abbreviation for Interlock Twist Yarn and is usually polyester. This common fabric is soft, has great drape, comes in a wide variety of prints, and is a good fabric to begin sewing knits with. The only downside is that it is usually 100% polyester and can look cheap, depending on the print. On the other hand, this fabric holds prints and wears very well, and a nice print will really make it stand out. ITY is a good choice for buying online since there is not much variance in quality.

MODAL, OR RAYON BLENDS

Modal is a type of rayon and is usually blended with spandex. I always look for a midweight that is not too heavy and not too sheer. I like around 92% rayon and 8% spandex. My favorites are slightly cool to the touch. Modal usually wears well, and is great for machine washing cold and line drying. This textile steams like a dream if it winds up getting wrinkled.

TYPES OF KNITS

COMMON LABEL	DESCRIPTION	POPULAR FIBERS	COMMON USES
JERSEY	SOFT, PLIABLE SINGLE YARN KNIT. INCLUDES SINGLE JERSEY, DOUBLE JERSEY, INTERLOCK JERSEY, AND JACQUARD JERSEY.	COTTON, WOOL, POLYESTER, RAYON, SILK, NYLON, SPANDEX BLENDS	DRESSES, TOPS, SKIRTS, LEGGINGS; COMMON ALL-PURPOSE KNIT FABRIC.
SPANDEX	ANY FABRIC WITH A HIGH (APPROXIMATELY 4%-20%) SPANDEX CONTENT.	SPANDEX BLENDED WITH POLYESTER, NYLON, RAYON, COTTON	SWIMWEAR, ACTIVEWEAR, CONTROL GARMENTS, COSTUMES, LINGERIE
RIBBED KNIT	A VERY STRETCHY FABRIC WITH RIDGES FORMED BY ALTERNATING KNIT AND PURL STITCHES. TIGHT RIBS ARE OFTEN USED FOR CUFFS AND NECKLINE BANDS.	COTTON, WOOL, POLYESTER, RAYON, SILK, NYLON, SPANDEX BLENDS	CUFFS, NECKLINE BANDS (TIGHT RIB); T-SHIRTS, TANK TOPS, DRESSES (LIGHT RIB)
TRICOT	A WARP KNIT FABRIC USUALLY USED FOR LINGERIE.	NYLON	SLIPS, UNDERWEAR, LINGERIE
LINGERIE	ANY FABRIC COMMONLY USED FOR LINGERIE, INCLUDING TRICOT, STRETCH LACE, LIGHT MESH, AND POWERMESH.	NYLON, POLYESTER, COTTON, SPANDEX BLENDS	SLIPS, UNDERWEAR, LINGERIE. CAN ALSO BE CREATIVELY USED IN DRESSES, TOPS, AND MORE
SWEATER KNIT	KNITS TYPICALLY CREATED WITH LARGER YARNS. CAN BE MADE IN A VARIETY OF TEXTURES AND WEIGHTS.	COTTON, WOOL, POLYESTER, RAYON, SILK, ACRYLIC, NYLON BLENDS, SPANDEX BLENDS	SWEATERS, DRESSES
FLEECE	KNIT FABRIC WITH A NAPPED OR BRUSHED BACK, INCLUDING SWEATSHIRT FLEECE, FRENCH TERRY, AND POLAR FLEECE.	COTTON, POLYESTER, ACRYLIC	SWEATSHIRTS, DRESSES, LEGGINGS
DOUBLE KNIT OR PONTE	DENSE, STRETCHY KNITS WITH GOOD RECOVERY.	COTTON, POLYESTER, WOOL, SPANDEX BLENDS	DRESSES, SKIRTS, PANTS. CAN BE SEWN MUCH LIKE A WOVEN FABRIC.
ITY	POLYESTER FABRIC WITH GOOD DRAPE AND A WIDE VARIETY OF PRINTS.	POLYESTER	DRESSES, SKIRTS
MODAL	RAYON BLEND FABRIC, USUALLY JERSEY. COMES IN A VARIETY OF WEIGHTS.	RAYON AND SPANDEX.	DRESSES, TOPS, SKIRTS, LEGGINGS. COMMON ALL-PURPOSE KNIT FABRIC.

My friend Chelsea and I are fabulous shopping partners because we are both super tactile. We love to touch everything we pass, just like little kids. I like to pull, stretch, tug, poke, and sift things between my fingers. If a fabric doesn't survive that, I usually don't want to play with it. I'm a little mean to my potential fabrics.

LOOK FOR LABELS

Depending on what fabric store you are visiting, you may find some bolts have plenty of information and some far too little. This is another reason I go around touching anything that catches my eye. Your store may have things neatly sorted and labeled for you, or just lumped together in one big knits area.

SHOP WITH YOUR HANDS

I love to touch garments, guess what the fabric content is, and then look at the tag to see if I was right. I've been doing it so long I can know modal in a split second. Comparison shopping and feeling ready-to-wear garments can be a great exercise if you need some inspiration or are unsure of where to start. This will give you great insight into what kinds of fabric will work well with different projects. In the corporate apparel industry, it is quite common to comparison shop to see what's working well for other companies.

I joke that I am mean to fabric when purchasing, but I always want to know what I am getting myself into. This is true not only in sewing the garment, but in wearing over time. To me, there is nothing more disappointing than working hard to make a lovely project only to have the fabric wear out quickly. In the past I've wound up in a pickle when, despite being unsure about the hand feel of a fabric, I purchased it anyway; I later found out that I also disliked wearing the fabric as a finished garment.

ROLLING

Any time I come across a knit I like, I walk right up to that roll, find the cut edge and give it a little tug. I take the fabric in both hands, around 3" apart, and pull gently until it won't stretch any further. All knits will roll, but this is a good time to determine how much rolling you want to deal with in your project. Often you will find more rolling on lightweight knits as opposed to heavier weight ones, but I never cease to be surprised.

STRETCH

You should stretch the fabric both vertically and horizontally to see how much give there is. I always favor fabrics that have stretch in both directions, and anything with some spandex should have plenty. Take the fabric in both hands, around 3" apart, and pull to see how far it will go. After that, poke the fabric with your finger and see how it returns. If the fabric leaves a nipple-like shape after this test, I usually pass on it.

VERTICAL GROWTH

If you have too much stretch in a fabric, or the weight is rather heavy, you can have a disproportionate amount of vertical growth in your garment. It may lay flat and measure correctly, but on a hanger or a body it will stretch and grow long. This is usually due to the weight of the garment, such as a skirt or dress that requires a yard or more of heavy fabric.

RECOVERY

After you tug on a fabric to check the stretch, it should return to its original shape. This is called recovery. If the fabric you are testing out has indentations from checking its vertical and horizontal stretch, that is an indicator to walk away. I find this most commonly on cottons without spandex.

PILLING

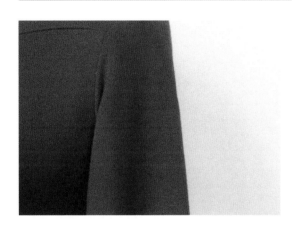

Pilling is not just for sweaters! I have seen fabric pilling on a bolt (and even sadder, on new dresses in stores). If a fabric is pilling on the bolt, put it down and walk away no matter how pretty, unless you really love using a sweater shaver. A quick way to test a fabric for pilling is to take a small corner of the fabric on the bolt and fold it over so the fabric is touching face to face. Quickly rub the fabric together for a few moments to simulate abrasion. If the face of your fabric changes drastically, that's a good indication to move on.

HAND FEEL

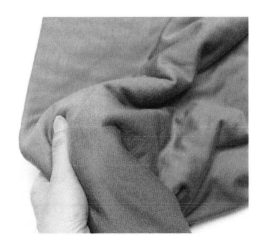

How does the fabric feel when you touch it? More importantly, do you want that feeling against your skin for a day? Hand feel is a preference thing, based on your own personal likes and dislikes. I've been called the "fabric snob" at some of my apparel industry jobs, as I have sensitive skin and didn't like the meshes or synthetics that were catching the skin on my fingers. There is no shortage of amazing fabrics out there, so don't settle on something you won't want to wear just because it might work or you like the print.

HOW MUCH SHOULD YOU BUY?

I was not so lovingly nicknamed "The Chainsaw" when I worked in an apparel factory after being known to hurriedly cut samples by hand when in a time crunch, so I like to err on the side of extra yardage. You may even want to buy twice as much fabric in order to sew a test version and check for fit (see Chapter 8). You will also need a little extra yardage for getting all the machines set up and tensioned correctly for your project.

CHECK YOUR WIDTH

Once you have found something you would like to use for your project and taken it to the cutting counter, remember to take a peek at the width. Knits are most commonly made in a 58" cuttable width, but can range from 45" to 72". You may need to do some quick calculating for your project and adjust the yardage depending on what you have selected.

BUYING EXTRA

I am of the "measure twice, cut once" school. I always buy at least $1/4$ yard overage, or even more if I'm doing something new. I use the extra for any mistakes I may make in cutting or sewing. If your fabric is not expensive, you may also want to buy extra for making a test garment. If it is a pricey fabric, look for a test fabric with similar stretch and weight. Keep in mind that every knit fabric is a little different, so doing a test version with your actual garment fabric is always ideal.

INTERFACING

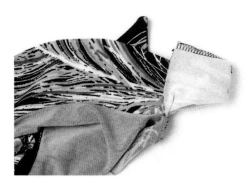

Knit interfacing is usually sold in the same area as other interfacings. It stretches along with your fabric, so it will stabilize the fabric but still have the mobility of a knit garment. It is mainly found in facings and plackets, just like you would see in a woven garment. Here, you can see it on the inside of a collar piece. If you are working on a project that calls for knit interfacing, always fuse it to the necessary pieces before beginning the project.

CHAPTER REVIEW

- Knits are created by knitting machines, while wovens are created on a loom.

- Knits get their stretch from their looped structure, and this is called mechanical stretch. They might also have yarn stretch if they contain spandex or elastane.

- Knit fabrics can be made from many types of fiber including cotton, polyester, silk, rayon, nylon, and wool.

- Knits can be labeled in many different ways at the fabric store.

- Shop with your hands and don't be afraid to test fabrics for rolling, stretch, and recovery.

- Don't forget to buy practice fabric. If possible, use the same fabric you'll be using in your final garment for your test garment, since every knit fabric behaves differently.

CHAPTER 2

NEEDLES AND THREAD

If you're new to sewing with knit fabrics, you may have noticed the large cones of thread at your fabric store and wondered how it's different from the small spools you are used to buying. In this chapter, we'll go over the different types of thread available, and how they compare to threads used to sew woven fabrics.

We'll also talk about the types of needles you should buy, and how to address problems that come up when your needle isn't the right fit for your fabric.

NEEDLES

As with any sewing, it is very important to select the correct size and type of needle for your project. Spending hours sewing only to realize your needles left puncture wounds in your fabric has to be one of the worst feelings in the world. Sometimes the wrong needle can even leave runs in knit fabric.

NEEDLE SIZE

The finer thread that is required to sew knits calls for using a finer needle. The size number gets larger as the needle gets larger.

NEEDLE TYPE

Look for needles labeled "jersey" or "ball pointed." These needles are designed to separate the threads of fabric rather than pierce them, so there's less chance of developing runs.

NEEDLE CHART

FABRIC TYPE	EXAMPLES	NEEDLE
VERY LIGHT	TISSUE THIN JERSEY, BURNOUT JERSEY, TISSUE THIN SWEATER KNIT	10/70 BALL-POINTED
LIGHT	T-SHIRT WEIGHT JERSEY, NYLON, ITY	11/75 OR 12/80 BALL-POINTED
MEDIUM	PONTE, DOUBLE KNIT, HEAVY JERSEY	12/80 OR 14/90 BALL-POINTED

NEEDLE ISSUES

If you use the incorrect needle with your knit project, bad things can happen. For example, the needle may puncture your fabric leaving a bunch of little holes instead of going between the fibers. There is no way to fix the holes, so select your needle wisely.

Not only can the wrong needle cause puncture holes, but in the worst case, it can actually cause the fabric to run! There is no fixing that problem other than starting over, or taking in your seams quite a bit. A little extra caution in choosing your needle can save you from some destroyed garments before they are even worn.

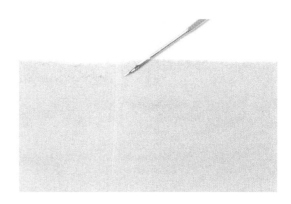

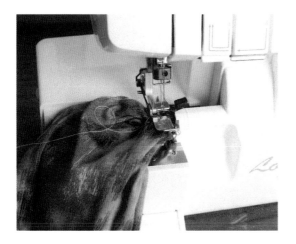

Using a needle that is too large can also cause fabric to be "eaten" by your machine. Instead of puncturing the fabric, the large needle just shoves it down into the machine. On the opposite end of the spectrum, a needle that is too small can cause your thread to break.

THREAD

Even if you've been sewing for a while, you may not have much experience with different types of thread. Just like with needles, it's important to choose the right weight for your project.

THREAD WEIGHT

Thread comes in many different weights. The unit of measure when talking about thread weight is called Tex. As the Tex number gets larger, the thread goes up in size. To find what size thread you are buying when at the store, turn your cone upside down and look inside. There is usually a sticker with order information and the Tex number.

Most thread that is sold at fabric stores on small spools is around Tex 35-40. This is a safe weight for sewing cotton wovens and any sort of home decor project. Depending on the brand of thread you are buying, the weight may be labeled.

TEX 18-30

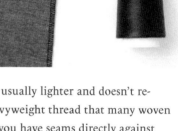

When sewing a knit fabric, the ideal Tex weight is anywhere from Tex 18 to Tex 30. Most of the thread in my studio is either Tex 24 or Tex 27. Maxilock is a common brand in fabric stores and comes in a wide variety of colors.

Knit fabric is usually lighter and doesn't require the heavyweight thread that many woven fabrics do. If you have seams directly against your skin, in your armpit, or any other sensitive place, you also want to make sure you don't feel any abrasion from the thread.

TEX 35-60

If you are doing a project on a serger and you would like heavier thread, you can sometimes buy Tex 40 and higher on cones. Use Tex 40 on wovens such as heavy curtains, denim, twill, or canvas for bags.

To give you an idea of where you may see different thread weights, inspect your wardrobe. Look at your knit items versus any denim you may have. Find two seams sewn on a serger and feel the difference. If you have any jeans with decorative stitching you may find that is a much denser thread and may even be Tex 60 or heavier!

BUYING CONES

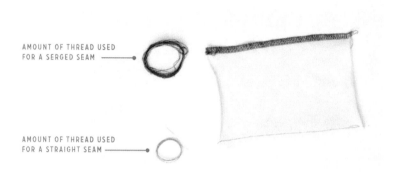

AMOUNT OF THREAD USED
FOR A SERGED SEAM

AMOUNT OF THREAD USED
FOR A STRAIGHT SEAM

For sewing knits, use cones of thread rather than spools. If you are sewing with a serger, you need the additional thread on the cone, since the loopers use much more thread than a regular home sewing machine. Here, you can see the amount of thread used sewing a seam with a straight stitch versus an overlock stitch on a serger.

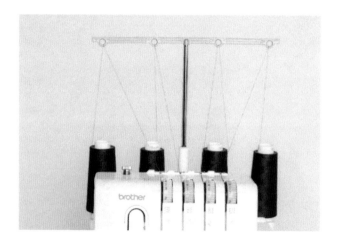

If you are sewing with a serger or other multi-needle machine, make sure all the cones of thread are the exact same weight. If they are not, it can create issues when sewing that cannot be solved by adjusting tension.

When I buy thread, I purchase 7 cones. 4 cones are for my serger, and 3 cones are for my coverstitch machine. If I set up for a project, one of my pet peeves is having to cut my cones and move from machine to machine. If you plan to use a coverstitch or serger alongside your regular sewing machine, plan accordingly when buying thread.

USING CONES ON A STANDARD SEWING MACHINE

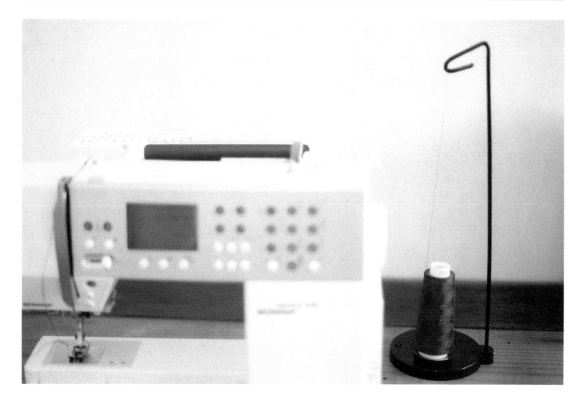

If you are cost-conscious about purchasing additional or different weights thread for projects, cones are the best option. It may be a little more expensive up front, but in the long run the cost per yard for thread is $1/4$ or less of what it would be on a spool. If you are sewing knits on a standard sewing machine, there is a fantastic device that holds your cone from behind the machine and feeds it up to the machine. Simply place the stand behind the machine, insert the cone, and thread as normal.

FLUFF THREAD

"Fluff" thread has a few different names; it might be called "fluff", "wooly nylon", or "texturized poly" thread. This is a thread I'd recommend if you are very concerned about abrasion on the seams of your garment, or you want a dense rolled hem on your serger. I prefer to use the general name "fluff thread" since other names refer to the fibers it is made out of.

Fluff thread can be made from either polyester or nylon and has a great deal of stretch due to the texture. It is also labeled in Tex weights, but Tex 35 is about as heavy as it goes, and that is rather dense. You can usually find this at your fabric store in a limited selection. Cones labeled "stretch thread" are also a form of fluff thread.

You will find fluff thread most commonly in lingerie garments, base layers, garments with flat seaming, or as a two thread narrow hem to finish garments. It is a great way to finish a seam on slips, or to use to create a lettuce edge.

Threading fluff thread can be tricky. One tip is to tie the end of your fluff thread to a piece of regular thread and use the regular thread to feed through the loopers. This will save you a ton of time, since feeding a mass of frizzy thread bits through a tiny hole truly does feel like mission impossible sometimes. For more information regarding tying on to thread a serger, see p.62.

CHAPTER REVIEW

- Look for ball pointed / jersey needles to avoid tearing knit fabrics.

- Choose an appropriate needle size for your fabric.

- Thread comes in different weights. A Tex 27 weight is common for sewing knits.

- Buying thread on cones instead of in spools saves you money, which is important because overlock stitches use much more thread than a straight stitch.

- Even if you don't have a serger, you can save money by buying thread on a cone and using a cone holding device with your sewing machine.

- Fluff thread (also called wooly nylon or texturized poly thread) is a good choice for areas that come in contact with the skin, such as in lingerie.

CHAPTER 3

NOTIONS AND TRIMS

If you haven't sewn much with knits before, you may not be used to all of the interesting and varied trims and notions that you can incorporate into your projects. Elastic is a particularly valuable trim when sewing with knit fabrics, since it stretches right along with the fabric. Other stretch trims are also available, and you can even experiment with non-stretch trims if you know where to place them.

We'll talk more about various ways to work with these trims in the techniques section of the book. For now, I'd like you to familiarize yourself with the kinds of knit trims that are available.

ELASTICS

One of the most common trims you'll use in sewing knits is elastic. Elastic may be a humble sort of trim, but its uses are varied when it comes to sewing knits. Because of its stretch, elastic is the perfect compliment to knit fabric and serves a variety of purposes.

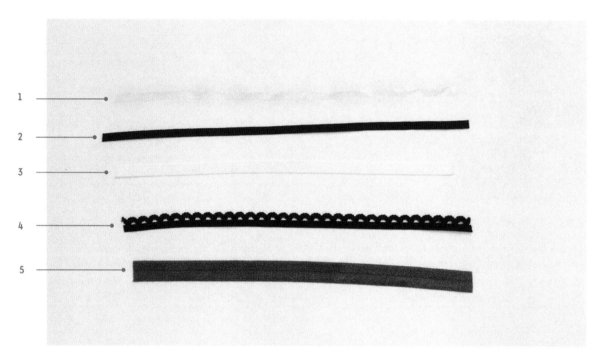

1. CLEAR ELASTIC	3. WOVEN ELASTIC	5. FOLD OVER ELASTIC
2. BRAIDED ELASTIC	4. DECORATIVE ELASTIC	

CLEAR ELASTIC

Clear elastic can be used in many ways in a knit garment. It works as a functioning elastic, a stabilizer, or both at once. Here, it's sewn into the waistband of a skirt to help create gathering. Learn how to use this technique by turning to page 128.

Clear elastic can also be used to stabilize seams to keep them from stretching out, such as in this shoulder seam. Ideally, you should buy clear elastic in a width that will be caught in your seam. For example, if your seam allowance is $^3/_8$" when finished, purchase $^1/_4$" wide elastic. Learn how to install clear elastic as a stabilizer by turning to page 127.

BRAIDED AND WOVEN ELASTIC

The terms "braided" and "woven" refer to the structure of the elastic. Test out the stretch of an elastic before committing to it. Some are stretchier or more dense than others. Your choice will be dictated by your use and where the elastic will be placed.

This type of elastic may also be installed within a seam like clear elastic, or it may be encased. Encased elastic is commonly found in waistbands. Tunneled elastic in a waistband creates lovely proportionate gathers.

This heavy elastic is great to use for waistlines, cuffs, and other areas that need a bit more stability. Sometimes they are even used as the waistband of a garment. In the garment seen here, a tube of knit fabric is simply sewn to a circle of wide elastic to create a simple skirt.

DECORATIVE AND LINGERIE ELASTIC

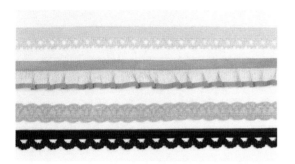

If an elastic is labeled for lingerie, don't be afraid to install it at a neckline, or use it as a lovely decorative finish. These elastics come in a few varieties, each with a unique look. See p.147 to learn how to install decorative elastic.

Elastic with one solid edge is often best for necklines. When shopping, check for a solid area $1/4$" to $3/8$" wide.

FOLD OVER ELASTIC

Fold over elastic is created with a fold down the middle, so that it can be folded and sewn over a raw edge in one step. It binds edges, much like bias tape would in a woven garment.

Fold over elastic makes a wonderful edge finish, and can add a bit of contrast to your garment. See p.146 to learn how to install this type of elastic.

OTHER TRIMS

In addition to elastic, there are a number of other trims that work particularly well with knit fabrics.

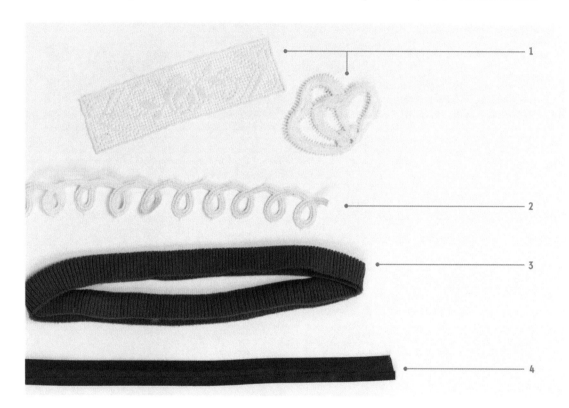

1. APPLIQUÉ

2. STRETCH LACE

3. RIBBING

4. FOLD OVER BINDING

FOLD OVER BINDING

Fold over binding is a great way to achieve a clean finish along an edge. If you have worked with bias tape or bindings in the past, the application is very similar. You can make your own from strips of fabric, or purchase it premade and folded like the binding in the picture to the left. You can also install it as a clean finish or seam covering binding. See pp.136-143 to learn more about these installation techniques.

RIBBING

You can purchase strips of ribbing, which can be sewn along edges to create a neat elastic finish. If you can't find ribbed edging, you can also cut strips of tightly ribbed fabric yourself. Install ribbing at a neckline or cuff by following the self fabric band technique on pp.132-135.

STRETCH LACE

Stretch laces, either in the form of continuous yardage or appliqués, are a fantastic way to add femininity to your garment. Lace can be added in a band, or used to create style lines, like these pieces on the left which are sewn at a 90 degree angle.

APPLIQUÉ

Some of my favorite forms of stretch appliqués are on slips and other undergarments, but I've had fun putting them in dresses as well. Simply zigzag around the edges to attach. For a little peek-a-boo, try cutting away the fabric from behind the appliqué (see p.152).

NON-STRETCH TRIMS

You can even use trims that do not have stretch. Reserve these trims for areas that don't need to stretch at all, such as a wide neckline, a full hem, or any area where a lack of stretch won't hinder getting into or out of the garment.

CHAPTER REVIEW

- Look primarily for trims that have stretch when sewing with knits.

- Clear elastic can be used as either a stabilizer, or as a functional elastic with shirring.

- Decorative elastic can be used to finish edges such as necklines, and doesn't need to be reserved for lingerie.

- Other types of elastic can be sewn directly to your garment or encased.

- Many stretch trims can be used to finish edges or add decorative touches.

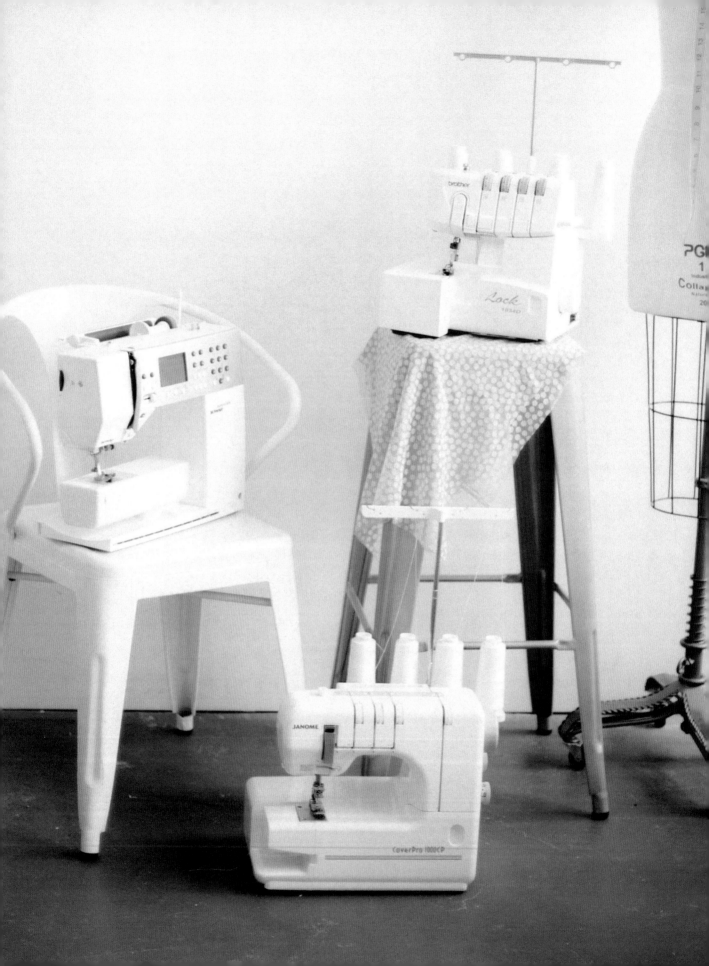

PART 2

MACHINES

CHAPTER 4

THE SERGER

My sewing life as I knew it completely changed when I learned how to use a serger. The straight stitch and I are still cordial pals, but the serger is my true love.

In this chapter, I'm going to get nerdy about knits. It may be a lot to absorb if you are new, but don't be afraid. I learned most of it through years of trial and error, and by re-threading sergers thousands of times. With a little experimentation of your own along with this chapter for reference, you'll have your own serger humming along soon.

Sergers can also be called overlock or overedge machines. For the sake of clarity, I will refer to the machines as sergers, but the stitch as overlock. Sergers can be used to sew together entire gar-

ments whether they're made from knits or wovens, or they can be used to finish edges. Home machines often have a few different stitches, whereas industrial machines each do one. If you are not well acquainted with your home serger, you may be amazed at all of the things it can do.

While a serger is the primary machine for sewing knits, you can still work with knits without one. Chapter 6 will discuss techniques using a home sewing machine, and the technique chapters in Part 3 will cover options for sewing with or without a serger whenever possible. If you fall in love with knits using your home sewing machine, investing in a serger may be the next logical step.

HOW THE SERGER WORKS

Let's start by taking a look at the mechanics of a serger. Compared to your regular sewing machine, there is more of everything!

In your regular sewing machine, the threaded needle goes up and down, catching thread from the bobbin to form a stitch. On the serger, there is no bobbin at all, and there is nothing to wind. Instead, there are loopers. These (you guessed it) form loops on your fabric. The stitches from the needle hold these loops in place.

The main complaint I hear about sergers is how complicated the insides seem. Each part has its specific function, and we'll go over them all together.

If you already own a serger, you may have seen some diagrams in your manual or even on the machine showing different stitches it can do. You can match them up with the numbers and images below.

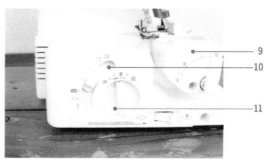

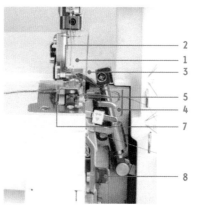

1. RIGHT NEEDLE	4. LOWER LOOPER	7. FEED DOGS	10. DIFFERENTIAL FEED DIAL
2. LEFT NEEDLE	5. CUTTING KNIFE	8. STITCH FINGER	11. STITCH LENGTH DIAL
3. UPPER LOOPER	6. TENSION DIALS	9. STITCH WIDTH DIAL	

NEEDLES

To start, let's talk about the simplest part and something you are already familiar with: the needles. Needles do the same thing on the serger that they do on your regular home sewing machine. They go up and down and connect with the looper thread the same way they do with your bobbin. Our needles are threaded here with yellow and green thread.

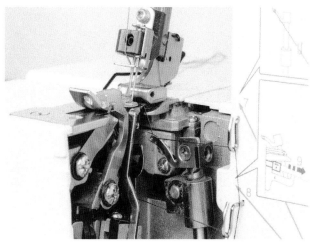

When the needles drop down below the feed dogs, they grab the thread from the loopers and pull it up.

UPPER LOOPER

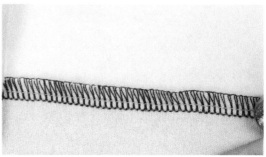

The upper looper (red) is the easier of the two loopers to thread. It is shorter in length and is the looper that pops up out of the machine and goes across the needles, hence the name upper. It is responsible for the loopy part of the stitch on the top of the sewing. Try turning the hand wheel of your serger and watch the upper looper move up and across.

Here you can see the top of the fabric. The red thread from the upper looper has created loops on top, held down by the needle threads.

LOWER LOOPER

The lower looper (blue) is often the hardest component of the machine to thread, due to how it moves within the machine. It loops back and forth underneath the feed dogs to create the loopy part of the stitch on the bottom of the sewing. If you look at your machine and move your hand wheel to simulate the stitching you can see how far this piece moves back and forth.

This is the bottom of the fabric. The lower looper has created the blue loops on the bottom, which are also held in place by the needle threads.

CUTTING KNIFE

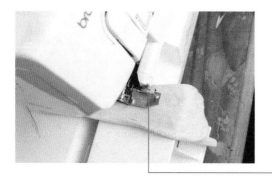

Along with all the business going on inside the serger, you also have a cutting knife, one of the best parts of sewing on a serger. The cutting knife trims your edges to perfection right next to your stitching, providing a neatly finished edge. Your serger will usually have a way to turn the cutting knife off when you don't need it. You might do this when sewing a tricky area, like a corner.

CUTTING KNIFE

TENSION DIALS

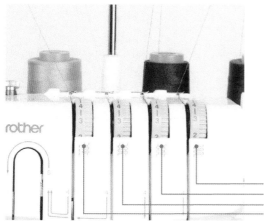

Tension dials may be familiar from your regular sewing machine, though they may look a little different on a serger. Many home sergers have numbers, which is extremely helpful for knowing where your tension is at all times. When you begin to sew, start with all of the dials on the same setting. Adjust as you do a test stitch on your fabric. Later in this chapter, I'll address troubleshooting tensions and how to adjust if you are encountering any issues.

LOWER LOOPER
UPPER LOOPER
RIGHT NEEDLE
LEFT NEEDLE

FEED DOGS

Feed dogs are the same as your regular sewing machine; they are what feed the fabric through as you are sewing. You may want to turn them up or down, depending on your fabric. The dial for this is most commonly located next to the hand wheel. Sometimes on finer knits, the feed dogs can leave marks, like a tire track in mud, so always test sew first. Near the feed dogs is a stitch finger which can usually be removed or disengaged for a tighter stitch, such as a rolled hem (see p.159).

FEED DOGS

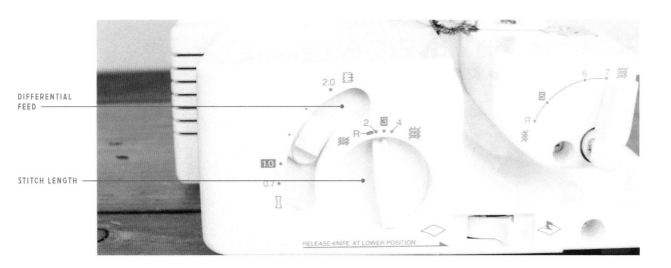

DIFFERENTIAL FEED

STITCH LENGTH

DIFFERENTIAL FEED

Differential feed controls the way fabric is fed through your machine. Turning it up means fabric is fed in more quickly than it is fed out, resulting in small gathers. Turning it down will stretch the fabric more as it's being sewn. If you find your fabric looks wavy after being sewn, it is likely being stretched too much while stitched. Try turning up your differential feed until the fabric lays flat.

STITCH LENGTH

Stitch length controls how many stitches per inch (SPI) the machine is achieving. To check the SPI on your stitching, you can quite literally can get out a ruler and count the stitches. You can do higher SPI for a denser stitch. The 10-12 SPI range is completely appropriate for most knit sewing projects. This translates to a 2-3 mm length on most sergers, like this one.

STITCH WIDTH

This controls how wide the loops are when sewing. You can adjust this by turning it up to produce a wider seam, or turning it down for a narrow seam. If you wanted to sew a narrow three thread overlock, you would remove the left needle and turn the stitch width down for a more narrow look (see p.64)

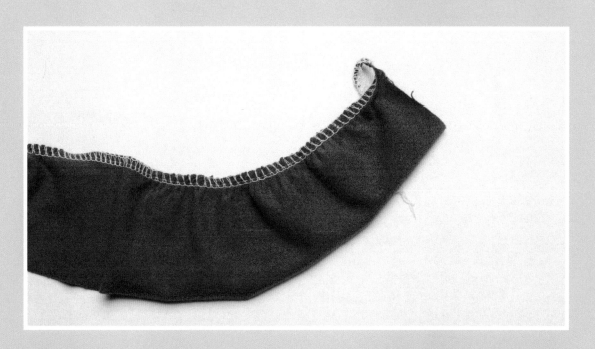

CREATING GATHERS USING DIFFERENTIAL FEED

The differential feed function makes it easy to create gathers, whether you're sewing knits or wovens. Simply turn the feed all the way up and fabric is fed under the needles more quickly than it is fed out, resulting in gathers. You may need to lengthen your stitches to 3-4mm to achieve gathers. Although you can't control the exact length after gathering like you can with hand shirring, this is a quick and easy way to create simple ruffles.

HOW TO THREAD THE SERGER

TIPS FOR THREADING

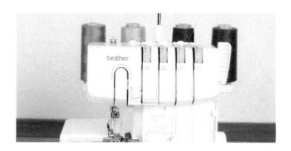

If you are new to serger tension and threading, start by threading each part with a different color. This will not only help you learn what each thread is doing in the stitch, but also allow you to easily identify which thread is your problem child if you do have any issues.

My best advice for threading is to get yourself a nice pair of tweezers. You will need them! I prefer a tweezer with an angled tip to get into the hard to reach areas.

THREAD THE NEEDLES

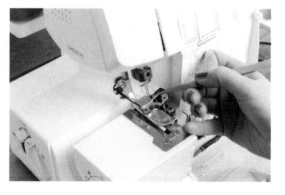

1. Consult your manual for detailed threading instructions for your machine. Here, we'll walk you through the basic steps. We will begin with the needles, because they're easiest to thread. Thread through the tension disc.

   Guide the thread through the thread channel above your needle. Make sure you can feel the dial grip your thread when pulling it through. If it's not in there, or even off to the side, it can make your stitching chain form incorrectly.

2. Once your thread is through the thread channel, thread the needle. Repeat for the second needle if you are using a two-needle machine.

3. Pull the threads to the back of the machine. This keeps them out of the way while you are threading the loopers.

THREAD UPPER LOOPER

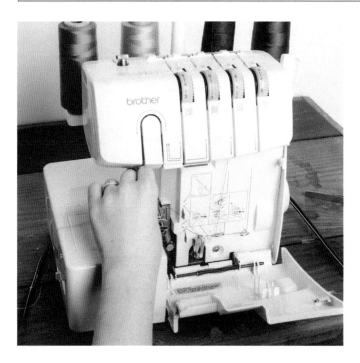

1. Next, we'll thread the upper looper. Start by feeding through the tension disc and down the thread channel. With the cover open, feed the thread through the thread guides on your machine in the order specified in your manual. Each serger is slightly different, but many have the sequence of threading labeled, like this one.

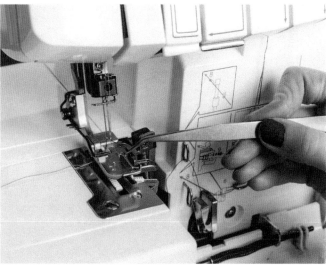

2. Thread through the eye in your upper looper, using tweezers. If necessary, you may turn the hand wheel so the upper looper is easier to thread. Once you have your looper threaded, pull the thread to the back of the machine in the same area as the needle threads.

THREAD LOWER LOOPER

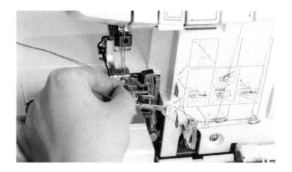

1. Finally, we'll thread the lower looper. Begin by threading through the tension discs and all thread guides on your machine.

2. For machines like this one (called "lay-in" machines), pull out the small threading lever and pull the thread around the lever.

3. Push the lever back in. If your machine does not have the lay-in threading feature, you will need to thread the lower looper manually. See the sidebar on p.61 for details.

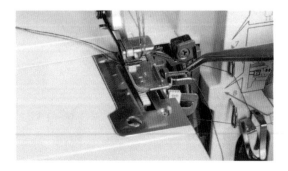

4. Feed the thread through the eye in the lower looper and pull the thread to the back. You are now ready to stitch.

THREADING THE LOWER LOOPER MANUALLY

If your serger does not have the handy threading lever of a lay-in machine, you will thread the lower looper manually instead. Begin by first threading the lower looper through the tension discs, thread channels, and thread guides on your machine.

1. Turn your hand wheel until the lower looper is all the way to the left. Use your tweezers to pull the thread through the machine and around the bend in the looper. Feed the thread through the groove or hook in your lower looper.

2. Feed the thread back through the machine, to the right.

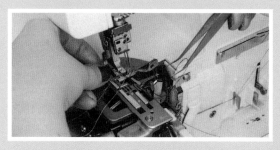

3. Use the hand wheel to move the looper to the right most position. As you are using the hand wheel to move, the thread will be trying to form a stitch. Use your tweezers to pull each thread out individually to prevent a stitch from forming. Pull all the threads to the back, like when you initially threaded the machine.

4. Once you have the thread back to the right side, thread through the other eye. If done correctly, your thread will now sit in the looper channel, and will not be caught or stuck on anything. Pull the thread up with the others, and you are ready to sew!

TYING ON

Remember that you don't have to thread and unthread like you would a normal sewing machine. Unless you love threading loopers, it is often much faster to use a tying on technique to change thread color than to completely rethread a multi-needled machine.

1. Trim each of your threads as close to the cone as possible.

2. Replace each of your cones with the new color, and tie the old thread ends to the new color. After you tie, give them a good tug to make sure the knot is tight.

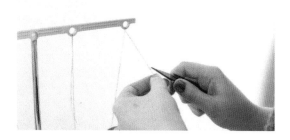

3. Trim each thread that hangs beyond the knot as close to the knot as possible. I find that a double knot work best; it's secure enough, but not too bulky to get caught on things.

4. Now look at the thread chain coming from the machine. I usually start with needle threads first as they are the easiest. Pull one thread at a time.

5. Once you feed the thread to the tension disc, lift your thread so the knot does not pass through the disc. Move the knot portion beyond the disc before reinserting the thread into the tension disc. This will prevent the knot from being caught in the disc.

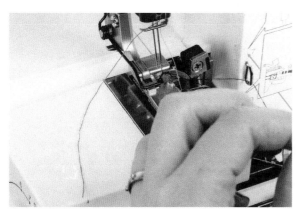

6. Continue to gently pull until you get the thread through the needle. If a break in the thread knot occurs, it's usually when pulling the thread through the needle hole. If it comes unknotted, this is the easiest part to re-thread. Be careful not to pull too hard or you may bend or break your needle. Here, you can see that the knot in the needle thread (green thread) has come undone, but can simply be threaded through the needle now.

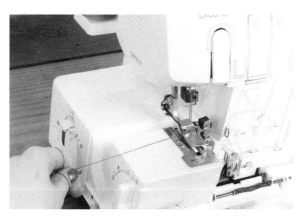

7. After you have threaded the needles, follow steps 4-6 with the looper threads. Once all the threads are pulled through, do a little sample stitching on some scrap fabric to make sure none of the tension settings on the machine need to be changed.

SERGER STITCHES

Now that we've talked about how a serger works and how to thread it, let's walk through the different stitches that a serger can do. Not all home machines are the same, so you may find that your machine can do all or just some of the things I talk about.

THREE THREAD ROLLED EDGE

This stitch uses both loopers and the right-hand needle thread. The stitch finger and left-hand needle are removed. The width and length of the stitch are lowered to create a very dense stitch. Refer to your manual for instructions on removing your stitch finger and the appropriate settings for your machine.

This is the back of the stitch, shown in blue thread. Mainly, you will see this stitch used as a contrast edge, as a lettuce hem, or as a finish on fine fabrics. It is commonly seen in lingerie. See p.159 for more on using this as a hem.

THREE THREAD OVERLOCK

This stitch uses one needle and two loopers. This can be used to finish edges or to sew fabrics together. I prefer to use a four thread stitch for putting most garments together, but this is a great stitch to use to sew a knit without much bulk. You can create a narrow three thread overlock by removing the left-hand needle and decreasing the stitch width. See serger stitches chart, p. 67.

The back of the stitch looks like this. Some examples of appropriate uses for this stitch would be in underwear, stitching on neckbands, or as a finish to stop unraveling if you have a loose or unruly fabric.

FOUR THREAD OVERLOCK

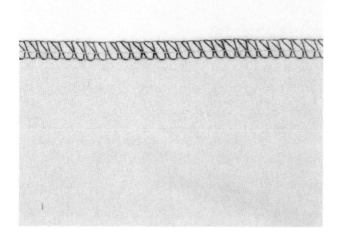

For this stitch, four threads are used: two for the needles and two for the loopers. This is the most secure stitch on most home sergers, and the one you will likely use for most projects.

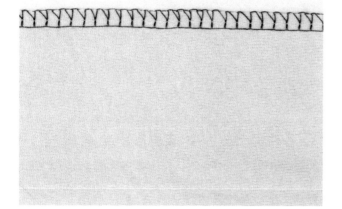

This stitch has looper threads connecting through both needle threads. Seam allowances can be $1/4"$ to $3/8"$, depending on your machine. These are the two most common seam allowances for knits.

FIVE THREAD SAFETY STITCH

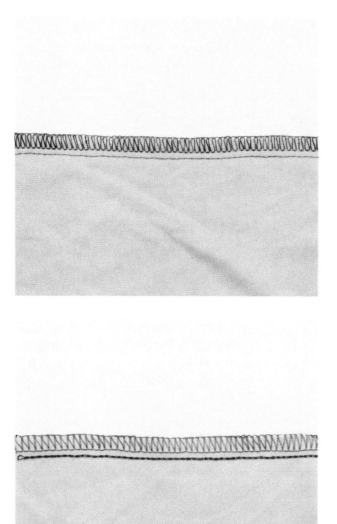

This stitch has two needles, but three loopers. It is extremely sturdy and secure. To create this stitch, you need a type of serger that has three loopers. Most home sergers have two.

This stitch is commonly used to sew wovens. Look for it on things like denim, tents, and heavy garments. You can use this on knits, but it is a bit of overkill. Also, the seam allowance on this stitch is usually ½", which is large for sewing knits.

SERGER STITCHES

STITCH NAME	NEEDLES USED	LOOPERS USED	STITCH WIDTH	STITCH LENGTH	USES
THREE THREAD ROLLED EDGE	RIGHT (REMOVE STITCH FINGER)	TWO	R (OR WIDTH RECOMMENDED IN YOUR SERGER MANUAL)	R (OR LENGTH RECOMMENDED IN YOUR SERGER MANUAL)	HEM, EDGE FINISH
THREE THREAD OVERLOCK	LEFT	TWO	5MM (OR WIDTH RECOMMENDED IN YOUR SERGER MANUAL)	2.5-3.0MM	SOMEWHAT NARROW, NON-BULKY SEAMS FOR AREAS THAT DO NOT HAVE HIGH STRESS. CAN ALSO BE USED AS A FINISH ON KNITS OR WOVENS TO STOP UNRAVELING.
NARROW THREE THREAD OVERLOCK	RIGHT	TWO	5MM (OR WIDTH RECOMMENDED IN YOUR SERGER MANUAL)	2.5-3.0MM	VERY NARROW, NON-BULKY SEAMS FOR UNDERWEAR, NECKBANDS, ETC.
FOUR THREAD OVERLOCK	RIGHT AND LEFT	TWO	5MM (OR WIDTH RECOMMENDED IN YOUR SERGER MANUAL)	2.5-3.0MM	STRONG SEAMS ON ALL GARMENT TYPES.
FIVE THREAD SAFETY STITCH	RIGHT AND LEFT	THREE (REQUIRES SPECIALIZED SERGER WITH THREE LOOPERS)	5.6MM (OR WIDTH RECOMMENDED IN YOUR SERGER MANUAL)	2.5-3.0MM	VERY STRONG SEAMS FOR HEAVY WOVENS, SUCH AS DENIM OR CANVAS.

If you already have your desired project fabric selected, use it for testing the thread tension. If you don't have your fabric yet, start with a stable cotton woven to give yourself a baseline for the machine.

Testing on actual fabric is something I cannot stress the importance of enough. Not only will it tell you if the tension on the machine itself is correct, but whether the tension is right for your particular fabric.

To test, stitch at least four inches. First, make sure that the thread is creating a proper stitch and thread chain. If not, open up your machine and make sure everything is threaded correctly.

Each thread can create its own issue if the tension is off. Below are some pictures for quick identification of issues and how to correct them. We'll begin with two examples to help you test your needle tension. We'll then look at the symptoms of improper upper or lower looper tension.

NEEDLE TENSION TEST 1: POPPING STITCHES

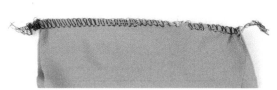

Needle threads can look fine to the naked eye only to show performance issues later with wear. First, stretch your stitch like you would stretch your fabric if you were testing it out at the store. If your tension is correct, you should get the same resistance from all threads of the stitch.

If you have any popping, it is almost always your needle thread. You should be able to feel and hear this. If one or both of your needle threads has popped, this means that your needle tension is too tight. Loosen one number at a time, and keep stitching until you are able to stretch your stitching without breaking. Nothing is worse than thread popping along the waistline of a garment!

NEEDLE TENSION TEST 2: GRIN THROUGH

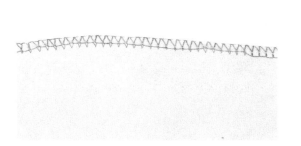

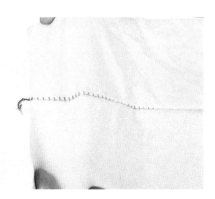

For this test, use two layers of fabric to simulate a seam. Sew a few inches, then take a look at the stitching. It may look fine when coming off the machine, but you still want to check this.

On the right sides, grab each side of the fabric and pull. Think about how much you anticipate stretching the garment in wearing. If you can see the stitches, this is called grin through and your needle thread tension is too loose. Try tightening your thread tension dials in small amounts until you can get this to stop happening. If you do a large jump to a higher tension, you may develop the first problem of tight needle threads and stitches popping.

FABRIC GRIN THROUGH

In the examples above, the term "grin through" means that your stitches are visible when the seam is stretched. But grin through is also a term that refers to printed fabric. This means that when a printed fabric is stretched, you can see the base color the fabric is printed on through the design. It can distort your print or cause it to look odd in some areas that are being stretched more than others, like the bust.

CHECKING LOOPER TENSION

UPPER LOOPER

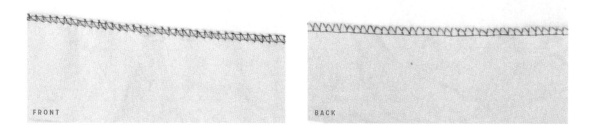

When the upper looper is too tight, you'll notice the upper looper threads (red) look too narrow, and are pulling on the lower looper (blue) threads. Try lowering the upper looper tension dial and test again.

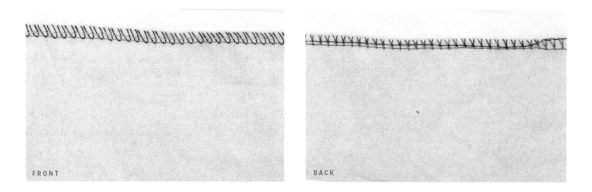

If the upper looper is too loose, the upper looper threads (red) wrap around to the underside of the fabric. The stitches appear loose. Try raising the upper looper tension.

LOWER LOOPER

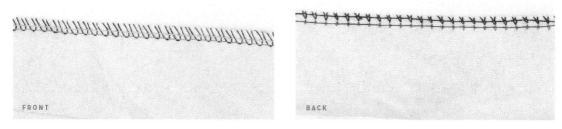

FRONT   BACK

If the lower looper is too tight, the lower looper threads (blue) pull the upper looper threads (red) to the underside. The stitches appear tight, and may pull on the edge of the fabric. Try lowering your lower looper tension.

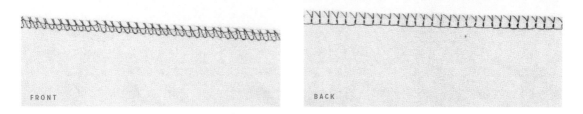

FRONT   BACK

If the lower looper is too loose, the lower looper threads (blue) wrap around to the top side of the fabric. The stitches appear loose. Try raising the lower looper tension.

KEEPING IT CLEAN

Machine crankiness can often be solved by removing any fiber build up in the machine. It is amazing how much fluff from both thread and fabric ends up in the feed dogs, loopers and cutting knife. Compressed air is used in industry settings, though some machine manufacturers recommend lint brushes or small vacuums.

TROUBLESHOOTING

Sometimes even all the correct threading and tensioning in the world cannot help if you have something mechanically out of whack with your machine. If you're frustrated by trying to tension or sew, these identifiers may help you decide whether it's time for a check up.

ISSUE 1: NOT ENOUGH TENSION

If you tighten the tension disc and still have grin through problems, the cause could be your tension discs themselves. Sometimes tension discs can lose tension over time. To test if this is an issue, make sure your thread is inserted properly through the tension discs and turn the dial to the highest setting. If you have no difference in resistance, your tension discs are having issues.

First, clear away any fibers that may have built up in this area. Then take a piece of dense fabric, such as denim or heavy twill. Trim the edge so you have a clean straight line without any threads hanging. Insert the fabric like you would the thread into the tension discs and move up and down. This will dislodge any other fibers or build up that are left. After cleaning, try rethreading the offending tension disc. If you are still having the same problem without any improvement it is time to take your machine in for servicing.

ISSUE 2: TIMING IS OFF WITH LOOPERS

This pesky problem can be difficult to identify. If the timing of one looper is off, it can mess up the stitch and thread chain. The result may be garbled rows of stitching, poor loop formation, or skipped stitches. If you feel confident that you have your machine threaded correctly but you cannot get a chain to form, take it in. If the timing is off, a tune up from a mechanic will take care of that.

ISSUE 3: METAL ON METAL

Just like your car breaks, the sound of metal grinding on metal is the worst thing to hear in your machine. If you hear clicking, grinding or metal noises, that is the cue to stop sewing and get your machine to the hospital as soon as possible. A broken looper is a much more costly repair than a tune up!

HOW TO GET YOUR SERGER SERVICED

If you take your machine for any type of service, make sure to take an example of the stitching problem on fabric to show the technician. There are many ways you can explain and describe something, but one sample is worth 1,000 words.

When you pick your machine up, take the time to test it in person at the shop. Nothing is worse than getting a machine home, only to find it is still having problems.

ISSUE 4: OLD NEEDLES

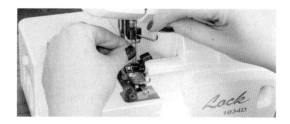

If you are sure you have your machine threaded correctly, the tensions are all correct, the machine is stitching, and you are still having trouble forming a stitch, there is one more possible culprit: your needles. Be sure to change your needles frequently. A worn out needle can cause all sorts of problems with both fabric and stitching.

CHAPTER REVIEW

- Sergers use a combination of needles, an upper looper, and a lower looper to stitch fabric together while finishing edges.

- The cutting knife on the serger trims fabric as you sew to create a neat edge.

- A pair of long, slanted tweezers makes threading the serger much easier.

- Differential feed controls the way fabric is fed into the machine and can be used to create gathers or keep fabric from getting stretched as it's sewn.

- To minimize time spent threading, try the "tying on" method when changing thread.

- The most common types of stitches you will use are the three thread rolled edge, three thread overlock, and four thread overlock. Some sergers can also do a five-thread safety stitch, which is more suited for wovens.

- Stitching problems can occur due to incorrect tension on the needles or the loopers. In other cases, your machine may require servicing.

CHAPTER 5

THE COVERSTITCH

After the serger, my next favorite machine is the coverstitch. Even if you are unfamiliar with the name, I am sure you've seen the end result.

If you own a t-shirt, take a look at the hem. You'll notice that it's finished on one side, with a double row of straight stitching on the other. This is created with a coverstitch machine, and this type of stitching is very common and extremely functional.

If you do not have a coverstitch machine or access to one, don't fret. There are plenty of other options. Some home serger machines have a large variety of stitches that include coverstitch as well as the chainstitch. Make sure to check your stitch guide. If your serger doesn't have

this functionality, you can replicate the stitches in other ways, most commonly with a twin needle on your home sewing machine (see p.92).

Whether you own a coverstitch or not, learning about their capabilities is instructive. It will give you a sense of how ready-to-wear clothing is constructed, so you can find ways to create the same look and function with the equipment you do have.

If you get familiar with knits and fall in love with them the way I have, a coverstitch might be a great investment after the serger.

HOW THE COVERSTITCH WORKS

When I first began sewing with this machine, there was a lot of cursing. In retrospect, I know it was because I didn't understand what the machine was doing and how the stitches were created. This machine is rather different from a regular sewing machine or even a serger.

1. RIGHT NEEDLE
2. CENTER NEEDLE
3. LEFT NEEDLE
4. LOOPER
5. TENSION DIALS
6. FEED DOGS
7. DIFFERENTIAL FEED DIAL
8. STITCH LENGTH

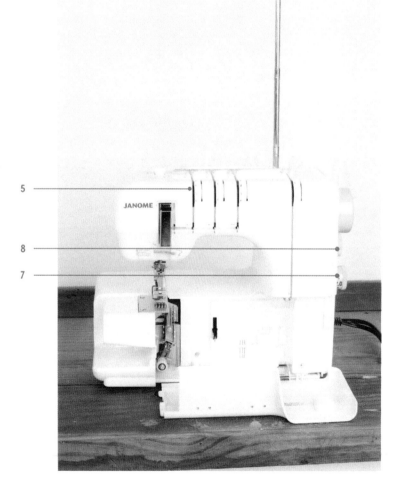

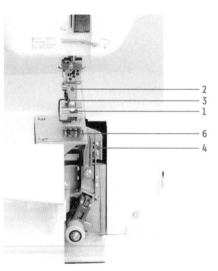

NEEDLES

The needle position of a coverstitch (or any multi-needle machine) is static. Your standard sewing machine may have the ability to move the needle position based on stitch and preference; but with a coverstitch, the loopers are counting on the needle or needles to be in the same place to properly join stitches. However, if you have a three needle machine, you can choose the width of your stitch depending on which needles you thread.

Just like on a serger, the needles drop down below the feed dogs and stitch the looper thread in place. The difference is that a coverstitch machine has two or three needles and only one looper. There is no upper looper, since there are no loops shown on the top of your stitching.

LOOPER

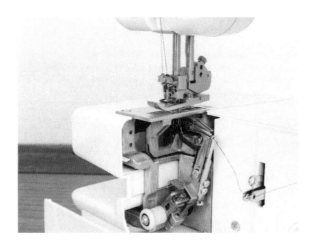

The looper thread is the only thread that is on the bottom of the stitch. The mechanics of the looper foot feed it through both the needle threads to create the stitch.

The looper can be threaded with the same weight of thread you are using for the needles, or with a texturized polyester or wooly nylon thread. This is often referred to as "fluff" thread (see p.36). You can make the choice based on your project. If you decide to use a regular spun thread, follow the same rule you would with the serger: make sure all the thread is the same weight. This will help prevent tension issues. In these photos, you can see the looper threaded with red.

If you think about what this is doing, it's pretty fantastic. The looper thread is not only forming a stitch with two needle threads, it is also looping to cover the raw edge of your fabric at the same time. Unlike the serger, there is no cutting knife to cut your fabric. This makes it perfect for creating neat folded hems.

FEED DOGS

Like with any other sewing machine, the feed dogs are responsible for pulling the fabric through as you sew.

DIFFERENTIAL FEED

Just like on a serger, the differential feed function lets you adjust the rate at which fabric is fed in and out as you stitch. If your fabric seems to be getting stretched out and creating wavy lines as you stitch, try adjusting the differential feed to slightly gather the fabric.

STITCH LENGTH

The stitch length dial controls the length of the stitches that are formed. Like a serger or your home sewing machine, you can adjust the stitch length.

TENSION DIALS

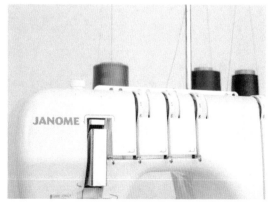

Like the serger, you can control the tension on each thread via the tension dials. Begin with all threads at the same tension setting and adjust from there as needed.

HOW TO THREAD THE COVERSTITCH

Understanding how to thread this machine takes a little time, but if you're familiar with threading a serger, it should be easy to get the hang of. Because there's only one looper to thread, it's a little easier than the serger.

THREAD THE NEEDLES

1. For each needle, feed the thread from the cone to the tension disc, making sure all threads are in the correct places. Feed thread through the thread channel above the needle. You may use either two needles (shown here in green and blue) or three needles if your machine has that capability. The third needle would go between the green and blue thread.

2. Feed thread down to the needles and insert into the hook above the needle to hold the thread in place. Thread through the eye of the needle for each needle thread and pull thread to the back.

CHANGING THREAD

To save time, you can change the thread on a coverstitch by tying on, just like a serger (see p.62). Trim each cone, tie on the new color, and feed it through. The only difference is that in this instance, you will pull your looper thread all the way through, since if you are re-threading, your looper thread will be coming out of your feed dogs.

THREAD THE LOOPER

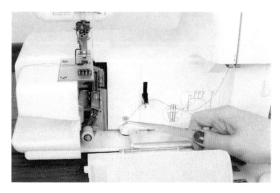

1. Now comes the slightly trickier part, the looper. It's a longer looper, which makes sense with all of the work it is doing. Unlike the serger, you do not see the looper in action while stitching. It lives inside the machine. To thread the looper, open the machine. Feed the thread through the tension dial, down the thread channel, and through the thread guides.

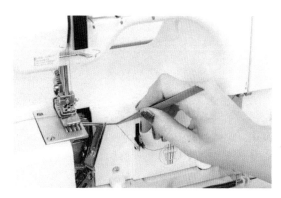

2. Use the hand wheel to get the looper as far as it will go to the right. This will give you the most access to the entire looper while threading. Thread through the first hole or channel in the looper.

3. Thread through the second channel in the looper. Brands vary, so if your coverstitch looper looks slightly different, consult your manual for more information.

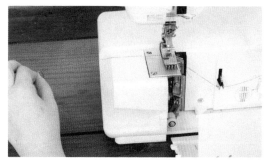

4. Once you have the looper threaded, leave that thread inside the machine. From the last looper hole, I usually pull about 2" of slack and let it lay in the machine. Since there is no bobbin, you will not pull the thread to link with the needle threads. This was extremely confusing for me starting out with this machine. I started out feeding the thread up between the feed dogs, which was very time consuming, and half the time unsuccessful.

STITCHING BASICS

The main reason I love this machine is that it hems and clean finishes the seam at the same time. I am a fan of any tool that saves time and makes things looks tidy when finished.

1. Position the needles above the presser foot. Use tweezers to feed the looper thread through the presser foot and behind the machine. Starting out like this will make sure the needles pick up your looper thread, and don't make any thread jams in the machine. Fold your fabric hem under and begin stitching.

2. The machine is set up to sew folded fabric with the outer portion on top and the raw edge of the hem on the bottom. The raw edge should be between the needles as you sew. You can use pins to hold the hem in place, but the best gauge is simply to feel the bump of the raw edge with your fingers as you sew, keeping it aligned between the needles, as shown.

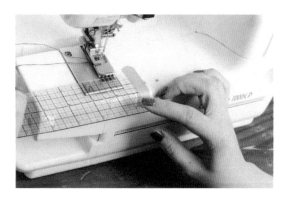

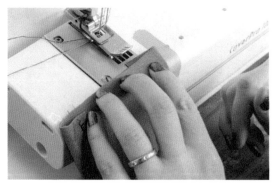

3. In commercial manufacturing, you would place a mark or tape on the side to show seam allowance and fold as you go. If you are pinning, make sure to remove pins before they reach the presser foot.

4. Your coverstitch presser foot should have small guide lines that are easily visible to you as you are sewing. If you find it hard to see them, get out that sharpie and make them easier to see. Place your fabric in the machine. The finished hem edge should line up with the tape, and the raw under edge should align with the center of the presser foot.

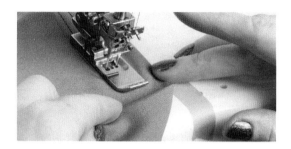

5. Begin stitching. Your machine will grab your looper thread as it stitches. This means the two needle threads will pick it up when you start and you can sew away. As you stitch, you will learn to feel with your hands that your fabric is centered and feeding at the center of your presser foot.

6. If your fabric does not stay between the markings, two things can happen. If it strays to the right, you will not catch your hem. If it strays to the left, you will have excess fabric sticking up above the stitch. This is more common and not the end of the world. You may go back after and trim down, but it will slightly change the length of your garment.

7. This machine does not chain off like a serger. When you reach the end of your stitching make sure to keep stitching over your starting area for at least 1".

8. To finish, make sure the needles are up, and manipulate the hand wheel when removing. Move the hand wheel backwards to give the thread and tension slack. Do not pull on the stitches coming from the garment when removing. This can loosen them or pull them out. Always grip from the stitches coming from your garment and pull away from the machine once you have manipulated the hand wheel. Trim the thread.

TWO NEEDLE COVERSTITCH STITCHES

TWO NEEDLE THREE THREAD COVERSTITCH

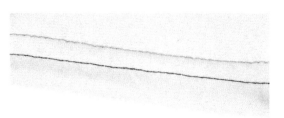 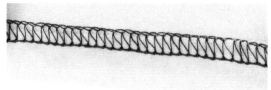

The most common stitch you will recognize from this machine is the two-needle three-thread stitching almost always found finishing t-shirts, knit dresses and tops, and often times hemming underwear. It stretches with the garment, making it a great choice for hemming most knits. This stitch has the look of two rows of stitching on the outside.

On the back of the stitch, you will see the loops from the looper thread (red). The looper on the bottom (usually the inside of garment) is what allows this stitch to stretch. Some machines have two needles and higher end models may have three. If you have a three needle machine, you are able to do a two needle coverstitch by removing the center needle.

CHAINSTITCH

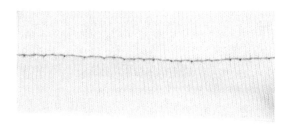 

The other fantastic thing a coverstitch machine can do is the chainstitch. On the outside, this may look like the regular straight stitch of a sewing machine, but that looper stitch on the back will be your best friend because it actually stretches. If you see what looks like a straight stitch on a ready to wear knit garment, take a closer look. It may, in fact, be a chainstitch.

It may not look like a lot, but that stretch in the looper thread (red) will allow you to achieve clean top stitching, understitching, install elastics, and create single needle hems in areas where stretch is a must for the function of the garment.

THREE NEEDLE COVERSTITCH STITCHES

If you have a machine that has 3 needles, you can also do a three row coverstitch.

THREE NEEDLE FOUR THREAD COVERSTITCH

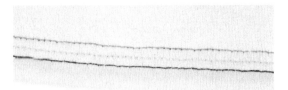 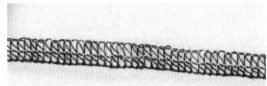

With a three needle machine, thread all three needles to create the three rows of stitching on top. In some cases, this can hold the fabric more securely in place while hemming, making it a good choice for shifting fabrics. You can see here that a third thread color has been added in the middle of the stitch (yellow).

The back of the three row stitch looks very similar to the two row stitch. The extra needle thread in the center helps to secure the looper thread even more.

CHAPTER REVIEW

- The coverstitch creates a finished edge on the underside of a hem with the look of two rows of straight stitching on top.

- The coverstitch has two or three needles but only one looper, which forms the loops on the underside of the fabric.

- The coverstitch does not cut your fabric as you sew, so you must handle your fabric carefully to keep your stitching even.

- You may choose to use pins when sewing a hem with the coverstitch, or use a piece of tape to guide the width of your hem.

- Use your fingers to feel the edge of the fabric on the underside as you sew.

- The coverstitch machine can do a two row or three row coverstitch, or a chainstitch.

- A chainstitch looks like a straight stitch from the right side, but has small loops on the wrong side that allow it to stretch.

CHAPTER 6

SEWING KNITS WITHOUT A SERGER

If sewing knits with a serger or coverstitch is not in the cards for you, you still have plenty of options with your standard home sewing machine. In fact, even if you have a serger, you may find yourself turning to your sewing machine for many tasks! Many machines come with an array of stitches that can be used with knits, the most common being the zigzag stitch. Other stitches imitate the look and functionality of the serger.

We are going to explore some of these stitches and how you might use them. As we get to the techniques later in the book, I'll provide options for using these stitches in place of a serger or a coverstitch machine.

STITCHES

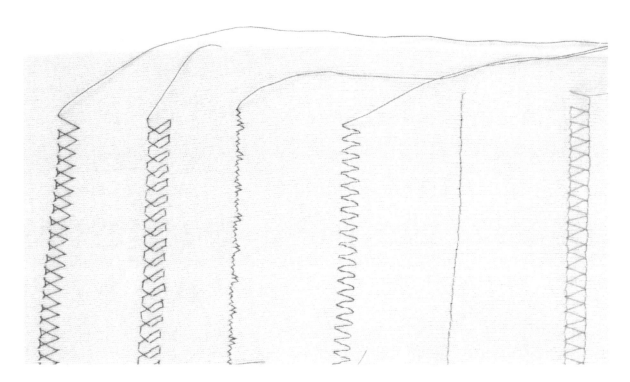

In commercial manufacturing, sewing knits usually means using a serger and a cover-stitch machine. But with all the methods and stitches available on home sewing machines today, you are by no means limited to using that kind of equipment. With a little experimentation, you can also sew beautiful knit garments with the machine you have.

THREE-STEP ZIGZAG

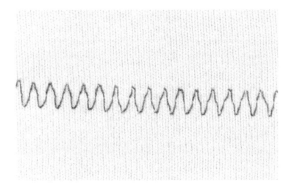

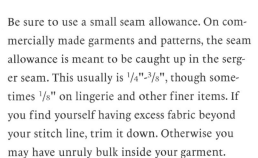

A three-step zigzag is a strong stitch that stretches well. It can be used for joining seams, or for installing elastic or doing topstitching. Each line of the zigzag is made by multiple stitches.

Be sure to use a small seam allowance. On commercially made garments and patterns, the seam allowance is meant to be caught up in the serger seam. This usually is $1/4"$-$3/8"$, though sometimes $1/8"$ on lingerie and other finer items. If you find yourself having excess fabric beyond your stitch line, trim it down. Otherwise you may have unruly bulk inside your garment.

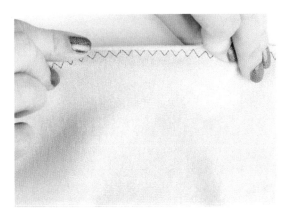

As always when sewing with knits, make sure your stitch stretches with your fabric without popping.

The zigzag stitch can also be used to create decorative stitches, as well as durable top stitching. You may find it on undergarments securing down elastic, or in a contrast color as a fun design element. See p.147 for more details on how the zigzag is used to secure elastic.

SINGLE-STEP ZIGZAG

The single-step zigzag stitch is extremely common on home machines, and it is also strong and stretchy. You can use it in much the same way as the three-step zigzag. For a narrow stitch that can be used for seams, use a stitch length of 2.5mm and a stitch width of 0.5mm. For a very narrow stitch that can be used for topstitching or edgestitching, use a length of 3.0mm and a width of 0.2mm.

MOCK OVERLOCK

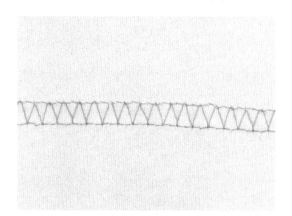

The mock overlock stitch replicates the look of the serger, finishing raw edges as you stitch. The mock overlock stitch can be used either to seam knit garments, or simply to finish seams and raw edges. You can even use it with your wovens to get a tidy look. Be aware that this stitch uses more thread than most, so you will go through spools quickly. Consider using a cone of thread with your sewing machine instead of the spools you are used to (see p. 35).

LIGHTNING STITCH

Some machines come with a stitch called the stretch stitch, or lightning stitch. As the name implies, it looks a bit like a lightning bolt and is a good choice for creating seams with stretch. It's an inconspicuous stitch that also works well for topstitching.

STRAIGHT STITCH

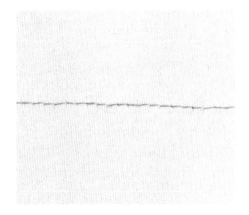

It is possible to sew knits with a regular straight stitch. But before you do, think about this: What would happen if you tried to put on briefs that didn't stretch where the elastic was? Or a swimsuit that had rigid stitching and didn't move with you in the water? How would you even get it on? What if you were putting on a t-shirt and as you pulled the neck over your head all the stitching popped, or it got stuck? This is why you are usually best off using a stitch that can stretch along with your fabric. Reserve use of the straight stitch for areas that require little to no stretch at all.

OTHER STITCHES

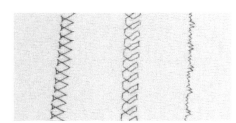

If you have a sewing machine with a lot of stitches, you may also have others that are intended to be used for sewing stretch fabrics. Take a look at your machine's manual to discover your options, then try a few of these out on knit fabrics to see which you like best.

SPECIALTY FEET

The trickiest thing about sewing knits on a standard home sewing machine is that knits are just not as stable. They tend to stretch and become pulled by the feed dogs when you sew.

To help with this, try using specialty feet that are designed to assist with the specific problems you'll encounter when sewing knits.

- **Walking foot:** The walking foot helps to feed fabric through your machine evenly as it's sewn. It grips the fabric and prevents it from shifting while being sewn.

- **Roller foot:** The roller foot is commonly used for leather, vinyl, and other sticky materials. But it can also help keep knits fed evenly while sewing.

- **Teflon coated foot:** The Teflon foot has a special coating and is a good choice when sewing with clear elastic because it prevents the elastic from sticking to the foot.

HEMMING WITH A TWIN NEEDLE

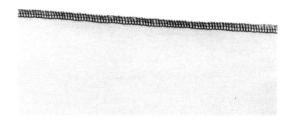

In the world of ready-to-wear, a coverstitch machine is usually used for creating neat hems with stretch. But you can still create that same look and functionality without a coverstitch, and even without a serger! All you need is a twin needle, a type of forked sewing machine needle that lets you sew two rows of stitching at once. Twin needles come in multiple widths. The wide width ($^1/_4$") will closely mimic the look of a coverstitch.

1. To start, finish the raw edge of your hem. You can use a serger to overlock the edge, or use your sewing machine's mock overlock stitch or a zigzag stitch to finish. While this step is not 100% necessary, it helps to create a cleaner and more durable edge.

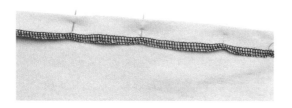

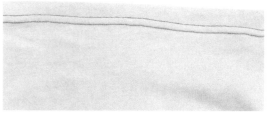

2. Turn the finished hem under and press into place. If possible, stabilize your hem with a product such as Wonder Tape (see sidebar, p. 93). Lower the bobbin tension to prevent the rows of stitches from forming a raised channel.

3. Insert the twin needle and follow your sewing machine's manual for threading it with two spools of thread. Stitch the hem in place with a straight stitch, catching and securing the raw edge beneath, just like a coverstitch. See pp.82-83 for tips on maintaining an even hem. The underside of the stitch will have a zigzag, allowing the stitches to stretch.

STABILIZING HEMS

Sometimes hems on knits can get a little wavy when they're sewn using the twin needle technique. This is usually because the fabric is being stretched a bit as it's sewn. To help get a crisp hem, try using a wash-away stabilizing tape, such as Wonder Tape. Wonder Tape is adhesive on both sides, so it even holds your hem in place while you sew!

Apply the tape to the wrong side of the fabric near the raw edge. Remove the backing, turn the hem up, and use the tape to adhere it in place. The tape will keep your hem in place while you sew, minimizing stretch, but will wash away later. Another option is a fusible interfacing tape, such as Stitch Witchery.

CHAPTER REVIEW

- Many home sewing machines come equipped with stitches that are appropriate for sewing knits.

- Common stitches used in sewing knits are the single-step zigzag, three-step zigzag, mock overlock, and lightning stitch.

- There are also many decorative and functional stitches available for knits on modern sewing machines. Check your manual for more information.

- To hem knits without a coverstitch machine try using a twin needle.

- Stabilizing tape can help keep your hem from becoming wavy and uneven.

PART 3

TECHNIQUES

CHAPTER 7

LAYING AND CUTTING

What is the best way to cut knits? The truth is, there isn't one correct answer. Everyone has different cutting tools they prefer, and you can usually mix and match depending on the fabric, the project, and your comfort level. If one method doesn't work well with your fabric, move on to another.

In this chapter, we'll discuss cutting tools you might want to try, and some of the special handling techniques you should be aware of when sewing with knits

TOOLS

The tools for cutting knits are very similar to the tools you use for cutting wovens. If you're used to sewing with wovens, you may still want to play around with different cutting methods.

The one thing to be aware of is that your fabric will try to move while you cut it. Knits are simply more mobile, and have a tendency to shift.

CUTTING WITH SHEARS

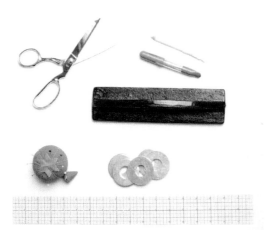

To cut with shears, you will need chalk or a washable fabric pen or pencil; pattern weights; and pins (optional). We'll cover how to cut with shears on p.104. These are the tools you will need.

 If you don't have a large surface for cutting, a quilting board is a great solution. This is ideal if you live in a small space. It's easy to tuck away behind a door or in a closet when not in use. You can even build your own cardboard surface! You can easily make it the width of your fabric, and the fabric and pattern can be pinned directly to it. Another option that works just as well is a bulletin board. This is great for securing patterns if you are doing pattern alterations, like changing dart placements or pivoting pieces.

CUTTING WITH A ROTARY CUTTER

Another option is cutting using a rotary cutter instead of shears. The rotary cutter is fast, and requires no tracing apart from transferring pattern markings. To use a rotary cutter, you will need chalk or a washable fabric pen or pencil; pattern weights; and a self-healing cutting mat.

Cutting with a rotary cutter requires a self-healing mat. This isn't the cheapest option, nor the smallest, but it is one of the quickest and most accurate once you get the hang of it. It also usually rolls up when not in use.

One fantastic thing about self-healing cutting mats is that they can be up to 59 inches wide. Knit fabrics are typically milled in the 57"-60" cuttable range, and sometimes even larger! This mat is ideal if you want to lay your fabric out for relaxing, or cut your pieces without folding your fabric in half. Many mats have markings on them as well, which makes them ideal for quilting and other projects.

TO PIN OR NOT TO PIN?

I find pinning a pattern in place very frustrating with knits. As you are pinning down your pattern, it is easy to skew your fabric as you are securing the pins around the piece. It can be aggravating to spend time getting your piece ready to cut only to notice your cutting is now a wobbly mess. I've had the displeasure of making quite a mess in cutting, and this ultimately makes sewing even more disastrous.

I prefer to hold pattern pieces in place with weights, then either trace my pattern or use a rotary cutter. This allows the fabric to naturally relax and lay as it would on its own. We'll walk through these methods beginning on p.104.

Patience is key when learning to cut knits, especially if you are used to stable wovens. You will definitely notice differences with the cutting and handling of the fabric. These techniques for laying out your fabric will help in minimizing frustration.

RELAX YOUR FABRIC

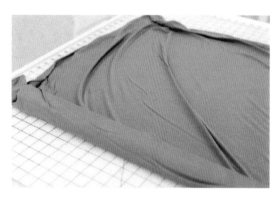

If your fabric has been wound tightly on a bolt at the time of purchase, relax it. Lay it flat, and let it sit for 24 hours. When fabric is milled, it can be stretched when winding on rolls and bolts. Relaxing the fabric will make sure it's in its final shape before cutting, since it literally relaxes back to its natural state. This is a common practice in the apparel industry.

Regardless of whether you went to the store and bought off a roll, ordered online, or purchased a pre-cut piece of fabric, a good rule of thumb is to let your fabric relax for 24 hours. If you did get it off of a roll, and you know it is high stretch, it's best to err on the side of 48 hours.

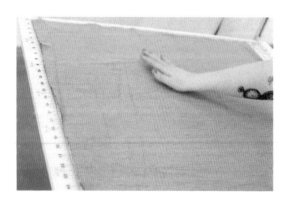

Ideally, you will lay your fabric out as you would cut it. If you will be cutting it on the fold, fold the right sides together with the selvage edges together along the length. Don't put any weights on it, or allow for it to hang.

DEALING WITH WRINKLES

Unless your fabric is extremely wrinkled, you do not need to press it. If you feel you have too many wrinkles, try steaming it instead. Pressing is much less valuable for knits than it is for wovens and it can sometimes stretch out the fabric. For the most part, in production sewing we go through sewing the entire garment without pressing; we just steam it once at the end. This is very different from wovens.

TRIMMING

You may find that the edges of your fabric are a bit skewed, and want to trim them to create a neat square or rectangle. Having uneven edges is much more common on knits than wovens, even along the selvage edges. A neat rectangle of fabric is much easier to work with.

LAYING

The right and wrong sides of knit fabric can sometimes be very clear, and other times almost impossible to tell apart. There is also not a rule on which way the fabric will be wound on a roll. The good news is, you can pick which side you would like to be the face. If you are using a fabric that has two sides, you may use that in your garment to add visual interest or color blocking. The garment will still work the same, regardless of the way you sew it. If you are able to tell the right side, but the right and the wrong sides are very similar, mark each cut piece on the wrong side while you are cutting. It is no fun to discover later that you have sewn one sleeve inside out.

FABRIC ROLLING

Fabric can roll both at the cut ends of the fabric and at the selvage, depending on the manufacturing process. In knits, not all selvages are created equally. Some are rolly hot messes, wrinkled, or even in squiggly lines. As long as you have enough cuttable width, it isn't anything to worry about.

LAYING ISSUES

As you begin laying out your fabric, you may notice some issues that make it hard to either lay or cut. Most of these are easily solved with a little trimming.

DISTORTED SELVAGE

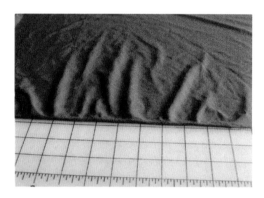

Sometimes, the selvage may be smaller than the rest of the fabric, resulting in wrinkles. It is difficult to get the fabric to lay flat towards the edges.

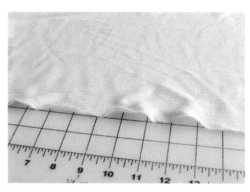

Other times, the selvage may be larger than the rest of the fabric, resulting in wavy lines. Both of these can be problematic.

If your selvage is really bothersome, don't be afraid to cut it off! Cut the fabric where the distortion ends, near the edge. If you are losing width in your cuttable area, make sure you still have enough yardage for your project.

MISALIGNED GRAIN

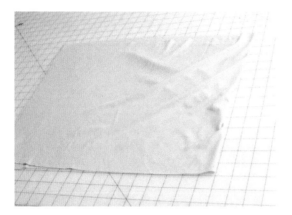

If your knit is wiggly and won't line up, don't try to align it by tugging on it. Pulling on a knit will not correct the grainline and may actually distort or stretch the knit. The fabric shown above may have a distorted grain line. This could stem from a manufacturing problem, the content of the fabric, or the knitting. You can still use this fabric, but let's get it more aligned before cutting.

1. Fold the fabric in half. Do this by lining up your selvages. Look at the fold line. If it looks like this, your grain is off in the fabric. It should be a clean line at the fold.

2. Hold your fabric along the fold. Shift the edges back and forth until you get a clean fold in your fabric. This fold is your grainline. If your fabric piece is too large to hold up, you can also do this with the fabric laying on the table.

3. After you have found the grainline, lay down your fabric. In addition to the uneven edges at the selvages, you will see an overlap on each of the cut ends. First, trim the selvage edges so that they are parallel to the foldline. Then trim your cut edges so they are 90 degrees to the fold.

HOW TO CUT

Now that we've gone over the tools you'll need and how to prepare your fabric for cutting, let's talk cutting methods. There are two methods I recommend. The first is cutting with fabric shears and the second uses a rotary cutter and self-healing cutting mat. Turn to pp.98-99 to see what tools you will need for each.

CUTTING WITH SHEARS

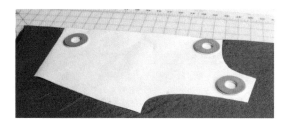 

1. Lay out the fabric on the cutting surface. Place the pattern pieces on the fabric and secure them with weights. Using chalk, fabric marker, or water soluble pencil, trace around each piece and transfer any pattern markings.

2. Remove the pattern pieces and begin cutting around the traced lines. Cut all of the straight away sections first. This will help you get a handle on cutting a straight line. If you are having trouble, you may try cutting out your curves after you have gotten the piece away from the main portion of the fabric. This will also increase your curve cutting accuracy.

CUTTING WITH A ROTARY CUTTER

To cut with a rotary cutter and mat, first lay the fabric on the mat. Place your pattern pieces and secure with weights. Use the rotary cutter to cut around the pattern pieces. Transfer any pattern markings using chalk, fabric pen, or water soluble pencil.

CLIPPING NOTCHES

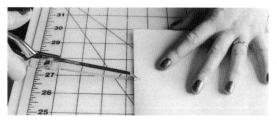

Whether you're using shears or a rotary, be sure to clip the notches. Clip directly in the center of the notch rather than cutting out a triangle. Keep in mind that since knits have a smaller seam allowance, you must be more conservative in your notching. If you are using a $1/4$" seam allowance, only notch $1/8$". It is not fun to sew something, and then realize you have a notch still going past your finished seam.

CUTTING ISSUES

Sometimes when cutting, you'll find that the threads aren't cutting cleanly. This happens to me often when I'm cutting fabric with spandex content because my cutting tool is cutting some of the fibers, but having a hard time with the tough spandex part of the yarn. This means that your cutting tool is not sharp enough. If you are using a rotary cutter, it's time to switch blades. With scissors, it means it is time to get them sharpened. If you are mid-project and sharpening is not an option at that moment, cut through the area again, until you can cut all of the threads. Make sure not to pull the threads with scissors or you may run your fabric.

Due to the wonderful mobility of knits, you can spend time getting your cut perfectly laid out and weighted only to have small areas move from a slight touch. If this is a serious issue, stabilizers can help to temporarily hold your fabric still. Stabilizers are available as spray-ons, or as wash away applications that look like interfacing. You may use them as you would in a woven. Always test a little piece and see how it reacts. Also check that you are fully able to remove the stabilizer by pressing or washing.

Knits will often roll after cutting. Not all fabrics are knitted equally, and some can be downright pesky. Don't be discouraged if you have selected a fabric that doesn't seem to roll, but suddenly rolls like crazy when you cut a 45 degree angle or curve. This does not mean you can't sew and make a great garment. Once your edge is sewn everything will be fine. If you really detest rolling, pay attention to the cut edge of fabric at the store. Pull on the edge a little to get an idea of what might happen when you actually work with it.

CHAPTER REVIEW

- Knits present some unique challenges when cutting due to their mobility.

- Knit fabrics can be cut with either tracing and shears, or with a rotary cutter and self-healing mat.

- Fabric should be relaxed before cutting to allow it to recover from being stretched on a roll.

- Distorted selvages on your fabric can be trimmed away.

- Uneven grainlines are common on knits but can be fixed by adjusting the fabric and trimming.

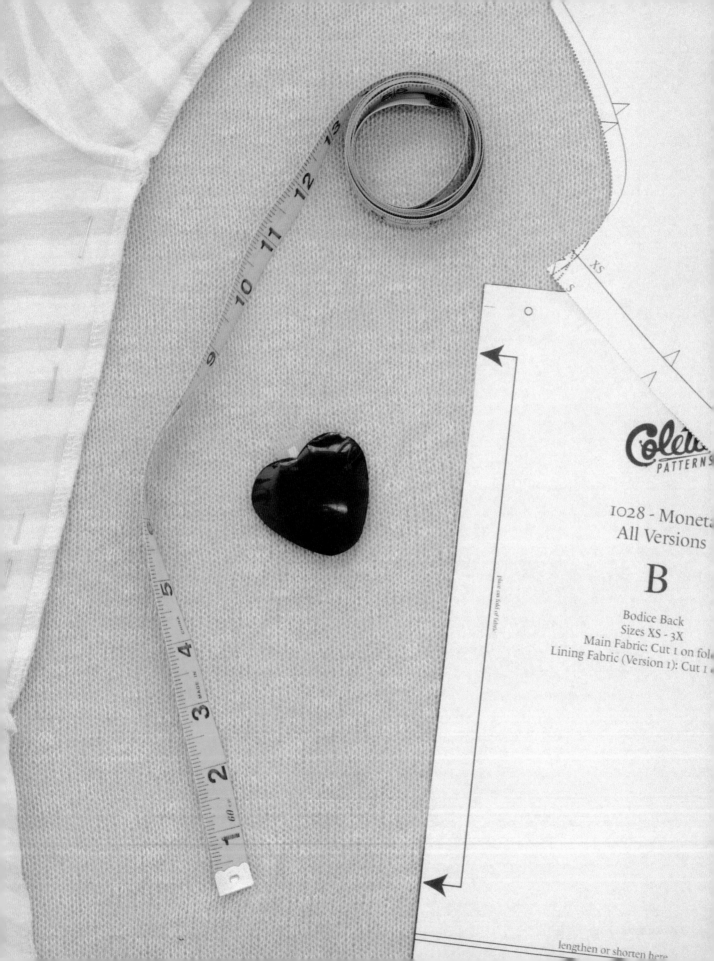

Colette
PATTERNS

1028 - Moneta
All Versions

B

Bodice Back
Sizes XS - 3X
Main Fabric: Cut 1 on fold
Lining Fabric (Version 1): Cut 1

place on fold of fabric

lengthen or shorten here

CHAPTER 8

FITTING

One of the many reasons I fell in love with sewing knits is how much fun it is to work with the patterns. After many years, I'm still learning new things as fabric technologies evolve and projects broaden. I think you'll find that playing with patterns and knits is a rewarding experience, like a little science experiment. You will learn from each project you tackle, because each project is a little different.

Fitting with knits is much easier in some ways. Because the fabric has stretch, the measurements do not need to be as precise to still achieve a fitted look. And because knits usually do not have darts, shaping is less complicated.

The downside is that each knit is different, so what works well in one fabric may not fit the same in another. For that reason, quick fit techniques often work best because you can fit as you sew. It's also handy to buy extra fabric and consider your first version a wearable test garment.

I was trained in working with structured wovens, so some of the differences between knit and woven patterns were a bit alarming to me at first. For one thing, knits move and stretch, which means the patterns do not always have to be as precise in conforming to the body as a woven. The fabric does some of that work for you!

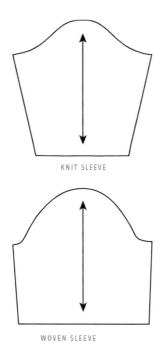

KNIT SLEEVE

WOVEN SLEEVE

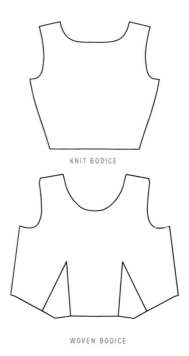

KNIT BODICE

WOVEN BODICE

The strangest thing to me when working in knits for the first time was the sleeve patterns. More often than not, the sleeves are symmetrical. Armholes can also be symmetrical. This went against everything I'd learned about fitting and drafting wovens, which are usually built with extra fabric at the back of the sleeve cap and less at the front. Knit sleeves are much simpler in shape.

Another big difference is darts; or more precisely, the lack of them. They simply aren't needed in knit patterns. With the stretch of the fabric, you can get the same degree of fit without them. If you see darts in knit garments, they may just be there for looks, not function. Instead, the fitting is usually done in the shape of the seams of the garment, often the side seams. The only exception might be garments made with very stable knits like a double knit, which can act a bit more like wovens.

EASE

Ease also differs in knits. Depending on your preferred fit and style of garment, ease may be small or non-existent. What this means is that the pattern of a knit garment may be the same size or even smaller than your body, depending on the style.

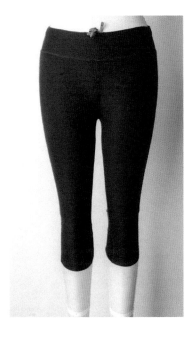

Some knit clothing fits snug to the body, with the textile stretching as you wear it. In fact, your garment may be doing this without you even knowing it! Control garments, underwear, and activewear are all examples of clothing that have **negative ease**, meaning it was patterned with the knowledge that it will grow when worn.

Fitted garments like this have **no ease**. They will stretch and give, but do not have any excess fabric in them for movement. For example, the Colette Patterns Mabel skirt is constructed of knit fabric so it does not have to have built in ease in order to be comfortable.

The garment shown here has **positive ease**, similar to a woven. Extra room is added to the pattern because it is not intended to hug the body.

QUICK FIT TECHNIQUES

One of the trickiest, and at times most frustrating, things about knits is that each fabric can behave differently. It is entirely possible to make two of the exact same garment in different fabrics and have the fit be completely different!

This is why you should always fit to your body as you work on a sewing project. This is a much better indicator than body measurements and pattern measurements when it comes to knits.

1. Construct the critical body seams to allow for trying on. On dresses and tops, join the side seams and shoulder seams; on skirts and pants, join waistbands and side seams.

2. Assess based on personal preference for ease and fit. Since knits don't have as large of a seam allowance as most woven patterns it is better to err on the side of making your garment a little larger and take away as needed.

3. Reduce as you desire. If you are using this to reduce your pattern, pin each side proportionally. That will give you a better idea of the final fit than only pinning one side.

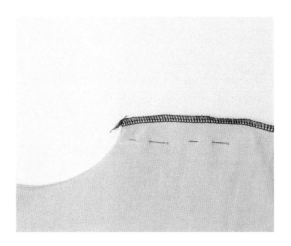

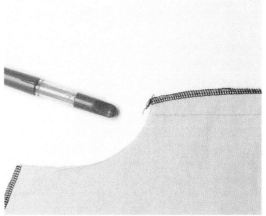

4. Check to make sure the reduction is the same. Or add the total together, divide in half and then reduce that amount on each side using pins.

5. Use a marking tool to mark the sewing line of the reduction.

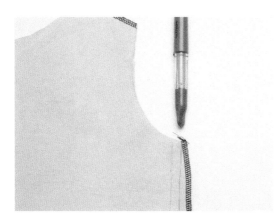

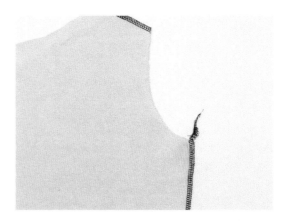

6. Optionally, mark the seam allowance next to the new seam line. This may help you feed the garment through a serger accurately.

7. Feed through your serger, removing excess with the cutting knife as you sew. Or if you are not feeling brave or are sewing without a serger, you can always trim down with scissors and then sew.

PATTERN ADJUSTMENTS

Sometimes, you may need to do more adjustments than simply removing ease. While knits are generally very easy to fit as you go, if you suspect that you might need specific adjustments, it is always wise to make a test garment.

Because every knit fabric is different, test garments should be made from the same fabric as your final garment. In other words, if you believe

you may need pattern adjustments, it's wise to buy extra fabric for testing. To save money and time, you can always test portions of your garment, such as creating a bodice rather than an entire dress.

Once you've made your test garment and measured the areas that need to be reduced or expanded, you must apply those adjustments to the pattern.

HOW TO MAKE ADJUSTMENTS

To lengthen or widen an area, draw a line straight through the pattern. Slash along this line, spread the pieces apart, and retrace the piece.

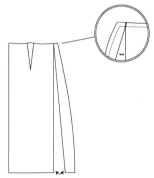

Sometimes, you may want to add or remove from an area without affecting the seamline. Draw a point on the seamline and slash only up to this point. Clip the seam allowance to create a tiny hinge. Pivot the pattern on this point to add or remove while keeping the seamline the same.

To shorten or narrow an area, again draw a line straight through the pattern. Fold along this line to remove length or width and tape in place.

To adjust some areas you may need to redraw curves. After measuring, use a curved ruler to taper curves back to the original seamline.

BUST ADJUSTMENT

It's far less common to adjust a knit pattern for a full bust than a woven pattern, since the fabric typically has enough stretch to accommodate a range of bust sizes. If you do need to adjust for a large bust on a knit pattern, you'll find that it is very different from using darts on a woven pattern, and hopefully a little more simple. Typically, the front and back of knit garments are very similar if not the same at the side seams, due to how knits stretch.

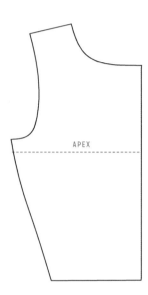 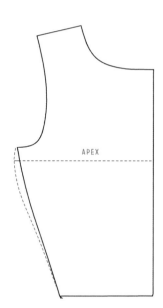

1. Determine the level of the apex of your bust by measuring your body. Mark this on the side seam. This will fall in a similar location to where a side seam bust dart would be. Add the needed width to the pattern at the point on the side seam.

2. Using a curved ruler, blend this point to your waist and underarm point, based on the size of your bust. The key is to keep the underarm point and waist the same. You may end up with a pattern that has a side seam with a slight "S" looking curve in it.

ADDING STYLE LINES FOR A FULL BUST

If your bust is very large or your knit fabric doesn't have enough stretch, another option is to add princess seams to your bodice, which can be manipulated to accommodate more fullness.

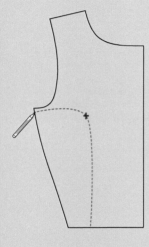

1. Identify the apex of your bust on the pattern piece. Draw a curved line from the side seam, through the apex, and down to the waist.

2. Cut the front bodice apart along this line to create two separate pattern pieces.

3. Add width at the apex on each piece, tapering toward the side seam and waist. Add in seam allowance on your new seams. You now have a princess style with added room at the bust.

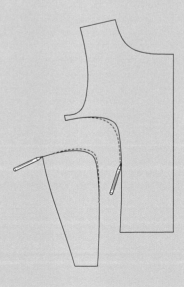

WAIST ADJUSTMENT

For waist adjustments, the key is to add or remove width from the waist without drastically changing the curve of the waistline or the length of other seams.

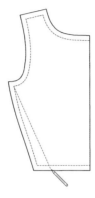

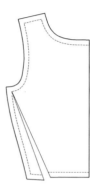

1. Begin by drawing in all seam allowances. Draw a line from the waist up to the underarm point on the seamline. Slash the pattern from the waist up to the underarm point.

2. Pivot the pattern from the underarm point, adding or removing width at the waist. Do the same for the bodice back and retrace all pieces.

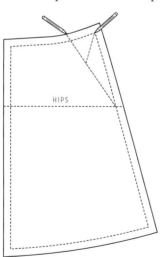

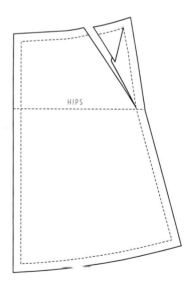

3. On a skirt piece, begin by drawing in all seam allowances. Draw a line indicating where your hips fall. Draw a line from where the hip line meets the side seam up to the waist. Draw another line from this line to the waist side seam point.

4. Slash the pattern from the waist to the hip point. Slash from this line up to the side seam waist point. Pivot the first line to add or remove width at the waist. Pivot the second line to straighten the waist and maintain the waist curve. Do the same for the skirt back and retrace all pieces.

HIP ADJUSTMENT

Adjusting the hips of a skirt is an easy alteration. Keep in mind that this simple method will also add width to the hem of your skirt. If you'd like to maintain the same hem width, complete this alteration, then redraw the curve of the side seam and blend back towards your original hem width.

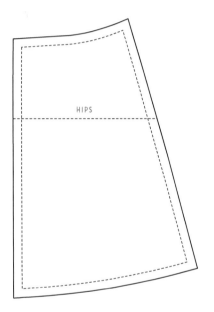

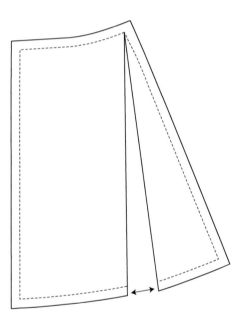

1. Begin by drawing in all seam allowances. Next, draw in your hip line on the skirt. Draw a line from the hem to the waist side seam point.

2. Slash along the line up to the waist side seam point. Pivot the piece in or out to add or remove width at the hip line. Do the same for the skirt back and retrace all pieces.

SHOULDER ADJUSTMENT

The key to a proper shoulder adjustment is widening or narrowing the shoulders without affecting the shape and size of the armhole. You'll see below that it's actually quite similar to the waist adjustments.

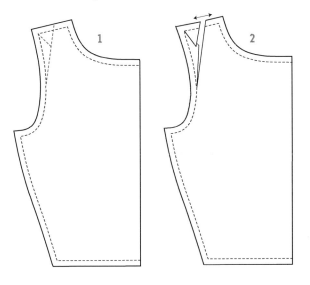

1. Begin by drawing in all seam allowances. Mark a point mid way down the armhole along the seam. Draw a line from this point to the shoulder seam. Draw a second line from the first line to the low shoulder point.

2. Slash the pattern from the shoulder to the armhole point. Slash from this line up to the low shoulder point. Pivot the first line to add or remove width at the shoulder. Pivot the second line to straighten the shoulder and maintain the original shoulder line. Do the same for the bodice back and retrace all pieces.

CHAPTER REVIEW

- Knit patterns are different from wovens in a number of ways. Most important, knit patterns rarely have darts and instead get their shape from the seams and the stretch of the fabric.

- Knit patterns are often symmetrical, whereas woven patterns are shaped differently at the front and back of armholes, sleeve caps, and waistlines.

- Much of the fit of a knit garment depends on the fabric and its stretch.

Each fabric will behave differently.

- Purchase extra fabric so that you can make test garments. To save money, create partial test garments for the most important fit areas, such as bodices.

- Use quick fit techniques to try on a garment and adjust as you sew.

- Make changes to pattern pieces by redrawing curves, or using the slash and spread or pivot methods.

CHAPTER 9

STITCHING AND FINISHING

Once you have your fabric cut and you feel confident about the fit it's time to get stitching! In this chapter we'll cover the basics of stitching and seaming, along with many techniques you can use to finish the edges of your garment. You'll learn several ways to create beautiful armholes, necklines, and more. We'll also cover techniques for using various trims and embellishments, including an array of elastics.

STITCHING AND SEAMING

If you're used to sewing wovens on your home sewing machine you'll notice some important differences when putting together knit garments. We'll go over a few methods of seaming, both with and without a serger. For a refresher on the serger, turn to chapter 4; to review stitches you can use without a serger, turn to chapter 6.

SEAMING WITH A SERGER

With a serger, you don't need to pull the on the thread to get a few extra inches before you start stitching. When you finish sewing a seam, keep your foot on the pedal to create a thread trail. Trim, leaving at least ½" still coming out of the machine in the stitch formation. This keeps the thread from being pulled back into the machine and helps avoid unnecessary re-threading. Do not pull on the thread when cutting or removing your garment from the machine.

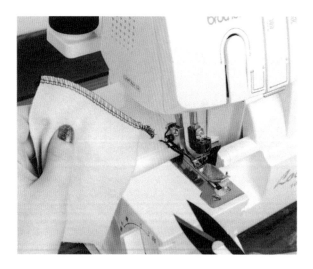

A best practice is to leave about an inch of thread tail on your garment when sewing with a serger. If you have a machine with a thread trimmer, this is about the distance it will cut to. As you continue sewing your garment, the thread tail will become encased in another seam or hem.

SERGING INTO A CORNER

Sewing corners will also be different with a serger. If you are sewing a heart shaped bodice, a chevron, a color blocked triangle shape, or scallops, you will need to do the stitching in two steps. Since you are sewing with a lot more thread, and possibly needles, pivoting at a corner becomes much more tricky than with a simple straight stitch. For this technique, you will need careful and precise handling to keep your fabric from being cut. Keep a close eye on your cutting knife while sewing, or disengage it while you sew.

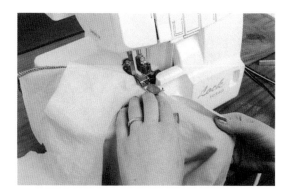

1. Begin sewing your seam as you normally would. Stitch towards the corner as you sew your two pieces together.

2. When you get near to the corner, move your fabric to keep it clear of the cutting knife, as shown.

3. Stitch off to give yourself a thread trail. Remove sewing from machine. You now have one half of the corner sewn

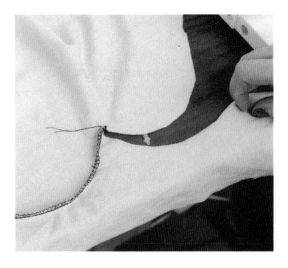

4. Rearrange your sewing so the seams are aligned.

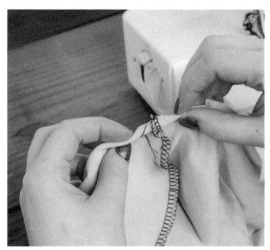

5. With right sides together, pinch the remaining corner seams together, beginning where your stitching ended.

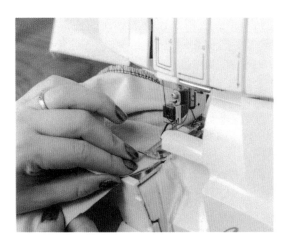

6. Beginning from the corner, stitch the remaining seam together. Be sure to stitch over the thread tail at the corner to secure it.

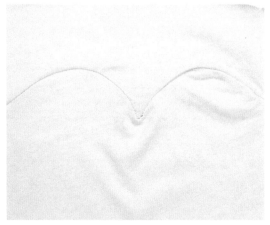

7. Your corner, scallop, or sweetheart seam is now complete. You may wish to practice this method several times before attempting it with a garment.

SEAMING WITHOUT A SERGER

If you want to seam a knit garment without a serger you have many stitch options. A zigzag stitch creates enough stretch to sew knits, but is still strong. Nearly all sewing machines will have a single-step zigzag, and most also have a three-step zigzag. Another option is the mock overlock stitch, shown here. Stitch right along edge for a quick and perfect seam. See pp.88-91 for more information on these stitches.

If your fabric is thin or unstable, your sewing machine may have difficulty sewing along the edge. This can result in your fabric becoming mangled and eaten by the machine.

If this happens to you, stitch away from the edge and then trim the seam allowance down for a finished look. You may need to adjust your seam allowances to provide more room for stitching and trimming; always test stitch some fabric before cutting.

RIPPING OUT

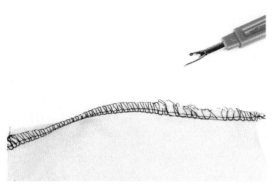

Ripping out serged seams can be a real pain, but with the right technique you'll find it's not much different from ripping any other seam. Grab your trusty seam ripper and start with the needle thread. Even though the loopy part is extremely tempting to tear into, unless you take out the needle part first, you'll just have a bunch of broken loops secured to your seam, as in this photo.

1. Place the seam face up; you will be able to see the stitches this way. If you still have your thread trail attached after sewing, you may start there. Begin with the left needle thread (green), as it is easy to grab since it is not next to stitching on one side. If you are starting on a seam that already had the thread chain trimmed, break a stitch with your seam ripper.

2. Once this is broken, go down a few stitches and loosen until you are able to pull the thread toward you. Do not break or rip the thread if possible. If you do, that's okay, but pulling the seam out this way is much more time consuming.

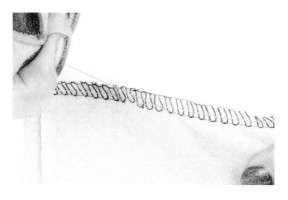

3. Once you feel you have enough to hold onto, grab your thread. If you have ever done hand shirring you'll find that this is a similar technique. Pull the thread as much as you are able and gather the seam of the garment. Do this as much as you can. If you have a short seam, often you can pull the entire thread without it breaking. If it is a longer seam, your thread may break and you'll have to repeat the process.

4. After you have removed all of the thread from this seam, your looper stitching will appear looser. Repeat the same process for the other needle thread. You will notice that your looper threads may start to fall away from the seam.

AVOID THREAD DISASTERS

When sewing with a serger, you should always try to avoid stitching over a seam more than once because it creates unnecessary bulk. It is also a terrible mess to rip out if you make a mistake, due to the amount of thread and overlapping stitches.

5. Once the needle threads are removed, it's easy to pull off the looper threads. I find it rather satisfying to pull all of the looper thread into a giant thread blob.

ELASTICS AND STABILIZERS

Elastics and knit fabrics go together like pea-nut butter and jelly. Because elastics are designed for stretch, they will have no prob-lem moving with your garment. They can be put to all kinds of interesting uses, from stabilizing seams to creating shirring.

CLEAR ELASTIC

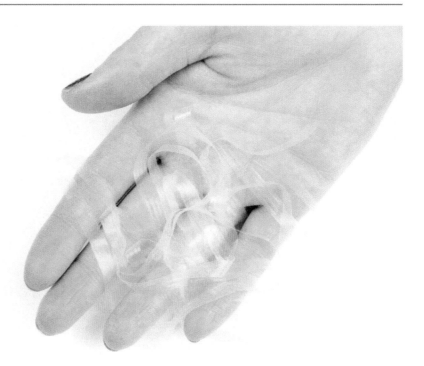

Clear elastic has many uses, but can be a little tricky to handle. When using it at home, allow yourself some patience while you get the position-ing correct. If you find the elastic is sticking to your presser foot, try using a special Teflon-coated foot. When clear elastic is installed in commercial manufacturing, it is done with a feeder foot, so the machine operator doesn't have to worry about keep-ing the correct tension or the elastic slipping. So if you become envious when you see that "perfect" elastic on a garment purchased from a large store, re-member that it was installed without a hand touch-ing it and a lot of help from special equipment.

STABILIZING WITH CLEAR ELASTIC

Clear elastic can be used to stabilize seams such as shoulders and necklines to prevent them from stretching out. I also put it in dresses that have waistlines that are tapered and will be stretched over shoulders and busts when put on. If you have a seam that will be stretched a lot and needs to maintain its shape, clear elastic will do the job. For this purpose, the elastic is installed in a 1:1 ratio with the fabric.

1. When purchasing clear elastic you should always buy more than you need. If a seam needs to be torn out it's better to start with a fresh piece. Clear elastic is neither knit or woven, so if you put a needle through it, it actually punctures the elastic. When sewing, leave excess on either end of the seam. Cutting the elastic the same length as the seam you are installing it to makes it very hard to handle at the beginning and end.

2. If you're installing clear elastic in a body seam it is not necessary to sew it in first and then sew the seam together. It is better to have less thread bulk and not stretch a seam by stitching on it more times than necessary. Arrange your sewing so that the clear elastic is either on the top of the fabric, or sandwiched between two layers. The important thing is to avoid contact between the elastic and the feed dogs.

3. Sew your seam, stitching over the clear elastic to secure it in the seam allowance. Sew as if it is one with the fabric, without stretching. If you are sewing a seam that is not closed on the ends make sure to leave some excess elastic behind the presser foot beyond the beginning of your seam.

4. Leave the excess at the end. Once you have sewn the seam and removed the piece, trim away excess elastic.

GATHERING WITH CLEAR ELASTIC

Clear elastic can also be used to gather fabric in places where you want a bit of shirring, much like any other elastic. There are two methods you can use for this.

METHOD 1: GATHER FIRST

1. If you are using clear elastic to gather as well stabilize, it is a good idea to gather first, and then stabilize. Use your sewing machine to create two rows of basting stitches. Pull the bobbin threads and adjust the fabric to create even gathers.

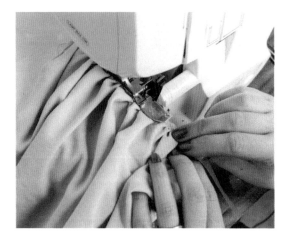

2. After gathering, install the clear elastic along the seam when putting the garment together, following the instructions on the previous page. As always, if you sew a gathered seam to a non-gathered seam, make sure the non-gathered seam is against the feed dogs while sewing. This is a great method for shirring and gathering perfectionists because you can see your distribution of gathers before committing to the seam. After you sew the seam with the clear elastic, remove your basting stitches, as they may pop when stretched.

METHOD 2: STRETCH AS YOU SEW

1. This method allows you to stretch as you sew (the elastic, not the fabric!). Mark the final length on the elastic with a marker. Leave a few inches of excess at the beginning and end of the elastic; this will provide you with something to hold on to as you are sewing.

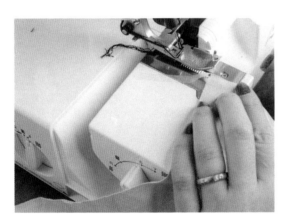

2. Align the first marked point with the edge of the fabric, or the place you would like the gathers to begin. Begin sewing a few stitches to secure.

3. Stretch the elastic as you sew, so that the second marked point aligns with the other edge of fabric, or the place you would like the gathers to end. For a proportionate distribution of gathers, do not let the tension on the elastic waver as you sew. If done correctly, the gathers will be even and your seam will be stabilized as well.

OTHER ELASTICS

In addition to clear elastic, there are several other types of elastic that can be applied to knits.

Braided and woven elastics can be installed much like clear elastic, or they can be encased in a fabric channel. Because these elastics are bulkier than clear elastic, they are less commonly used for simple shirring and stabilization.

Decorative elastics are commonly seen in lingerie, but they can be put to other uses as well. You can even use decorative elastic as an edge finish around a neckline or armhole! See p. 147 for instructions on installing this type of elastic.

STABILIZING TAPES

Stabilizing tapes are a quick and easy way to add sturdiness to a seam before sewing. They are useful for all areas that are prone to becoming overstretched. While clear elastic does a great job at stabilizing most tricky seams, such as waistlines, these tapes can also be useful for areas where the stretch of elastic isn't needed, such as wide hems or necklines.

Wash away stabilizing tapes add temporary stabilization to a seam. This makes it easier to sew areas that are prone to becoming stretched out while sewing, such as hems. Wonder Tape (shown here) is particularly useful for hems, as it is adhesive on both sides which allows you to fold, secure, and stabilize your hem all at once.

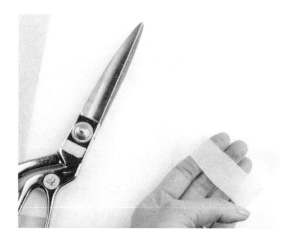

For more permanent stabilization, you can also cut strips of fusible knit interfacing. Use your iron to adhere the interfacing to areas that are prone to stretching out over time, such as shoulders or wide necklines. Interfacing strips allow you to make your own stabilizing tape at less cost. Be sure to use knit interfacing, which has some stretch.

EDGE FINISHES FOR NECKLINES, ARMHOLES, AND OPENINGS

The coverstitch machine (see Chapter 5) offers a quick and easy way to finish many edges, but it's certainly not the only option. Sometimes it's not even the best option! We are going to go over several different ways of finishing openings such as necklines and armholes. The main thing to remember is that any finish you choose should stretch along with your fabric.

SELF FABRIC BAND

A self fabric band is one of the simplest neckline finishes. Since you are using just a little bit of fabric you can almost always sneak in a piece without having to buy extra yardage. As an alternative, you can use a ribbed fabric in a matching color for a neckband (see p.135).

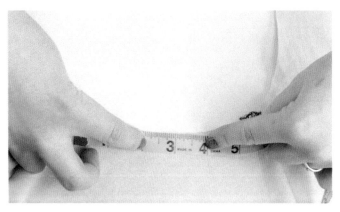

1. To start, measure the entire seam you want to install the self fabric band on. This measurement will serve as the starting point of the band. Next, determine the width you would like the band to be. $3/8$" to $5/8$" is a good starting point. Add seam allowance to this measurement. Double this number. This will be the width on the pattern piece you are making. For example, if you wanted to create a $3/8$" band with a $3/8$" seam allowance, your total width would be 1 $1/2$".

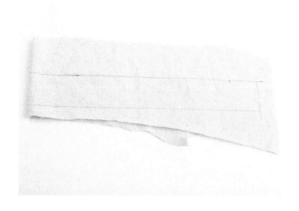

2. Draw a rectangle the length and width specified by your measurements. The grain will be
   the same as your garment. Draw the piece on
   the fold, as shown. For rib knits or high stretch
   fabrics, you may need to cut a band that is
   smaller than your neckline measurement. There
   is no exact measurement to reduce in length
   to get your band perfect. Don't be dismayed
   if you create one and it needs more fussing.

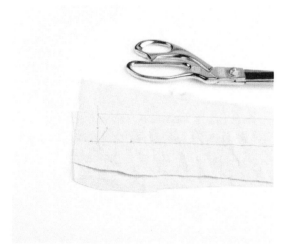

3. At the lengthwise center of your band, measure $^3/_8$"
   from the edge. From this point, draw lines toward
   each outer corner, as shown. The reason for this is
   that the circumference of your finished neck opening is decreasing towards the top of the band, so
   your neck or armhole will be slightly smaller once
   the band is installed.

4. Cut out the fabric piece, and join the sides
   together using an overlock or stretch stitch.

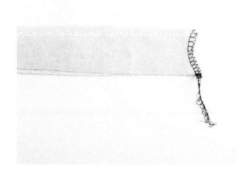

The band should now form a circle.

5. Fold the band in half lengthwise, with wrong sides together. Check and make sure the piece lays nicely. If the indentation at the side is either not enough or too severe it can lay oddly, and this can get worse once it's installed in your garment. This is the first check to make sure the piece will

work with the area it is being sewn into.

6. Once you have gotten to a satisfactory shape, select the location on the neckline where you would like the seam on your band. I usually pick center back, or line it up with the shoulder seam. Pin the band to the garment opening, with right sides together.

Check to make sure the band fits the garment. Pin the band into the neckline evenly.

7. With right sides together, stitch the band to the opening using a three-thread overlock, mock overlock, three-step zigzag, or single-step zigzag (see Stitch Chart, pp. 164-165). Once you have installed the band, your neckline will have a clean finish, with the stitching turned to the inside. If you'd like, you can topstitch around the neckline using a twin needle or chain-stitch to prevent the seam from rolling. This can be especially helpful when sewing narrow bands, which have a tendency to roll around.

TROUBLESHOOTING

Before sewing your band in, check to make sure it will fit without buckling or puckering. After you've pinned your band to the neckline but before you've stitched, look for these telltale signs of trouble.

If your neckline looks like this when you pin it, you may want to see if your band is too large for your garment. Remove the band and check measurements again. Another quick fix is to reduce your join seam until the neckline fits in well.

If your band makes your neckline pucker when pinned, the band is too small. It usually will not improve after sewing. Start over with drafting your band piece before sewing.

A RIBBED BAND

If you are working with a rib knit for your finishing, it may look somewhat puckered when pinned; you may have to adjust a little based on stretch. If your rib spreads a lot this may be okay. Do a test curve before actually installing it into your garment.

Take a look at a basic t-shirt or sweatshirt in your closet; you will see the rib knit is stretched slightly more in the neck seam of the garment than the center fold of the rib.

SELF FABRIC BINDING

Self fabric binding is very common in all sorts of ready to wear garments. Keep in mind that installing this in a manufacturing facility is very different than trying to accomplish it at home. In factories, fabric rolls are cut into strips, then fed through a folder foot and stitched on in one step. It works a bit differently without all that specialized equipment but you can still achieve the same effect.

You can do a self fabric binding in two ways, depending on how you want it to look on the outside of the garment. One is a clean finish binding, and the other is a seam covering binding. Both are good for adding stability around curved openings like necklines and armholes. Do be mindful of stretching out the binding and the curve when stitching them together. I also advise the use of an iron.

METHOD 1: CLEAN FINISH BINDING

On the outside of a garment with a clean finish binding, you will just see the stitch line. The binding is installed entirely on the interior of the garment.

METHOD 2: SEAM COVERING BINDING

Seam covering binding will be visible on the outside of the garment.

METHOD 1: CLEAN FINISH BINDING

1. First, cut out your binding. A finished width of $1/4$"- $3/8$" is a good guideline to use, as it is not too bulky, but wide enough to have some ease of handing. Add a seam allowance to this measurement. Double this number to get the width of your binding piece. For example, for a $3/8$" finished binding with $3/8$" seam allowances, cut a binding strip that is 1 $1/2$" wide. The length should be longer than your finished neckline.

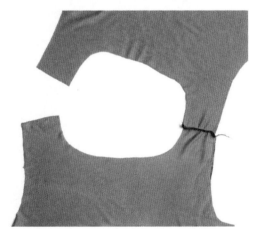

2. This type of binding is installed differently than a self-fabric band, which is sewn in the round. For easy sewing, leave one seam open on the body. For example, if you are binding a neckline, leave one shoulder seam open.

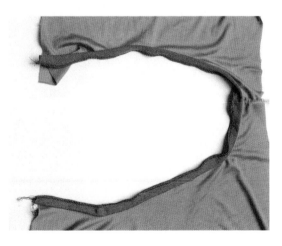

3. Fold the binding in half lengthwise, wrong sides together. With right sides together, align the raw edges of the folded binding strip with the raw edge of the neckline. Stitch the binding to the neckline, using a three-thread overlock, a mock overlock, a three-step zigzag, or a single-step zigzag (see Stitch Chart, pp. 164-165). Be sure not to stretch your fabric as you sew.

4. Close up the open seam in the body of the garment. Stitch the body seam, enclosing the entire binding like it is one with the seam.

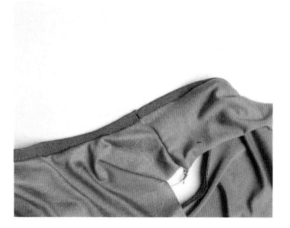

5. Reinforce the seam at the edge with a small bartack. To sew a bartack, set your machine to zigzag with a length of 0 and stitch back and forth several times, securing the seam allowance to the binding.

6. Turn the band to the inside. Use one of the edgestitching options (see sidebar) to secure the band in place. Now you will have a clean finished binding. The binding will show only on the inside of the garment. Ours is shown here in red for clarity, but you will likely make yours in the same fabric as your garment.

EDGESTITCHING OPTIONS

When installing a clean finish binding, you turn the binding to the inside of your garment and then secure it in place with edgestitching. For a seam covering binding, the binding is turned to the outside of the garment. Both must be secured with edgestitching. There are several ways you can do this. Here are three options.

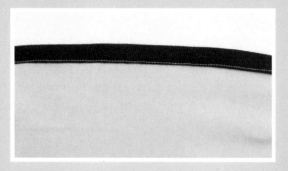

OPTION 1

If you have a coverstitch machine, use the chain-stitch to stitch around the neckline, holding the binding in place. For the clean finish option, stitch with the outside of the garment facing up, feeling for the edge of the binding with your hand. For the seam covering binding, edgestitch along the fold of the binding, as shown here.

OPTION 2

Using a twin needle, stitch the edge of the binding down. For the clean finish option, stitch with the outside of the garment facing up, feeling for the edge of the binding with your hand. For the seam covering binding, edgestitch along the fold of the binding, as shown here.

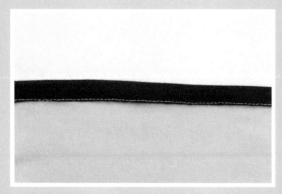

OPTION 3

You could also finish the edge with a single needle and a very narrow single-step zigzag (see Stitch Chart, p. 164-165). Alternately, you could use a straight stitch, but I would only advise this on larger openings that do not require a lot of stretch to get into. Using a contrast color thread can also look very nice.

METHOD 2: SEAM COVERING BINDING

A seam covering binding looks much like a bias tape finish on a woven garment, but is sewn differently. Depending on what you are making you can use it as a style detail as well.

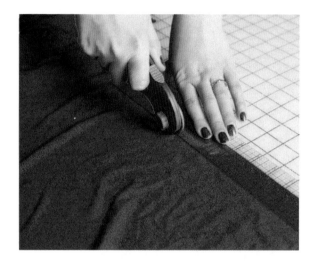

1. First, cut out your binding. Just like the clean finish binding (p. 136), a finished width of $1/4$"- $3/8$" is common. Add a seam allowance to this measurement. Double this number to get the width of your binding piece. For example, for a $3/8$" finished binding with $3/8$" seam allowances, cut a binding strip that is 1 $1/2$" wide. The length should be longer than your finished neckline.

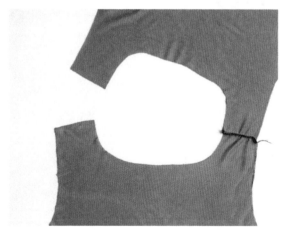

2. Like the clean finish binding (p. 136), leave one seam open on the body. For example, if you are binding a neckline, leave one shoulder seam open.

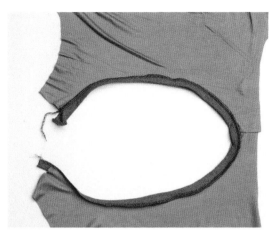

3. Fold the binding in half lengthwise, wrong sides together. With the binding on the wrong side of the garment, align the raw edges of the folded binding strip with the raw edge of the neckline. The seam allowance will be to the outside of the garment. Stitch the binding to the neckline using a three thread overlock, a mock overlock, a three-step zigzag, or a single-step zigzag (see Stitch Chart, p. 164-165). Be sure not to stretch your fabric as you sew.

4. Give the binding a light pressing to help it lay in place. Turn the binding to the outside of the garment, enclosing the seam allowance. Press and pin the binding into place.

5. Secure the binding by edgestitching along the fold. For edgestitching options, see the sidebar on p.139.

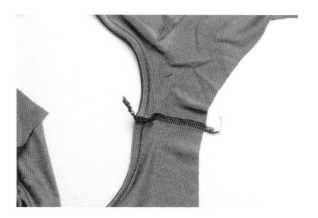

6. Once you have finished the opening, you need to close the body seam. Stitch the body seam, enclosing the entire binding as if it was one with the seam.

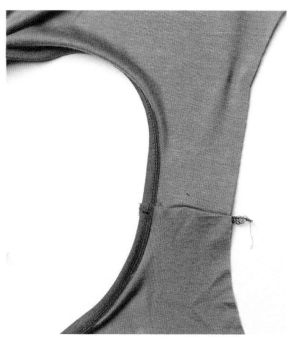

7. Turn the seam allowance down towards the fabric to secure. Reinforce the seam at the edge with a small bartack.

8. You have now completed your binding!

USING STRIPES

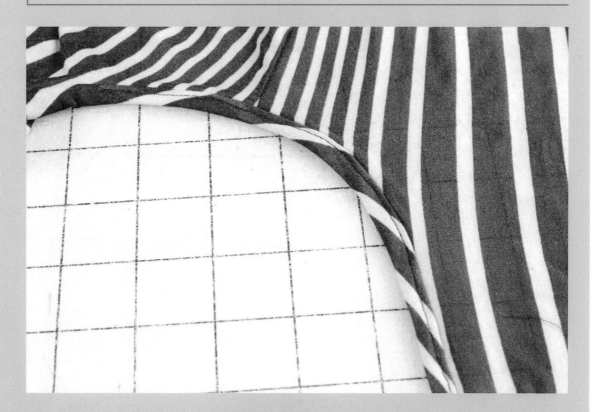

Cutting stripes on a different grain is a fun way to add some detail to a neckline.

RAW EDGE ROLLING BAND

This technique has been popular on ready to wear for the last few years. It adds some dimension to a neckline with simple steps. It's also great for utilizing leftover areas of your fabric.

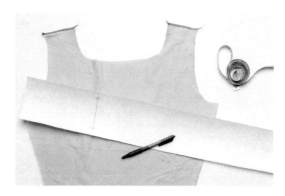

1. To start, measure the neckline of your garment, so that you have a base measurement for length. Now determine the desired width of the band; 1 to 1 $\frac{1}{2}$" is a good starting place. Add in seam allowance only on the bottom edge, as the top is a raw edge. Using theses measurements, draft your piece on paper.

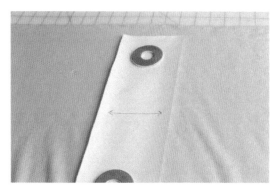

2. When you cut your fabric, make sure the length of the piece is on the grain with the most stretch. Usually, this means the short ends of the piece should be parallel to the selvage.

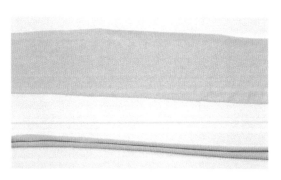

3. Give your fabric piece a tug to see the roll. Once you've stretched your fabric, trim the length of the piece once again so that it is 10% smaller than the neckline measurement. The fabric will be rolling to the right side. With right sides together, join the side seams of the band and stitch together to form a circular band.

4. Lay the band and the garment right sides together to stitch on. The seam will be on the inside of the garment. Pin if necessary for even installation. Stitch the band to the neckline using a three-thread overlock, mock overlock, single-step zigzag, or three-step zigzag (see Stitch Chart, pp.164-165), stretching the band slightly as you sew. Flip the band up and allow the fabric to roll towards the seam.

ROLLING BAND VARIATIONS

This is a fun one of play with. If you have scraps of favorite fabrics, try them out here. I have a special soft spot for fancy silks, and this is great way to add a pop of color to a solid garment.

Since the edge is not finished, it may fray after many washings, but that can also be part of the look. A woven fabric can be cut on the bias and frayed for a textured effect.

You can also add two or more colors of fabric at different widths for a more noticeable finish. The variations are endless.

5. If you prefer, you can also add topstitching to hold down the bulk of the seam allowance. For topstitching, use a chainstitch, twin needle, very narrow single-step zigzag, or lightning stitch (see Stitch Chart, pp.164-165). Topstitching is always helpful if your seam allowance is bulky or not laying flat.

FOLD OVER ELASTIC

If you are a fan of bias tape or bias binding, this may be the right finish for you. Fold over elastics are often found in lingerie items, but they are also great to use as a decorative finish on any edge of a knit garment. There is a large variety available and my favorites are usually found on spools in the lingerie sections of fabric stores.

1. If you are installing fold over elastic as a seam finish, leave one seam open. That way, there will be less bulk at the seam. For this example, we are finishing the waist of a skirt and have sewn only one side seam closed.

2. Fold the elastic in half and wrap it around the raw edge. Pin the elastic to the seam, leaving a few inches of extra at each end. Make sure you have your elastic evenly distributed. For a standard finish with no shirring, do not stretch your elastic as you install it. Edgestitch the elastic in place using a chainstitch, twin needle, very narrow single-step zigzag, or lightning stitch (see Stitch Chart, pp.164-165), catching both sides of the elastic as you stitch.

3. With right sides together, stitch the remaining body seam closed, enclosing the entire binding as if it is one with the seam. Use an overlock, mock overlock, 3-step zigzag, or single-step zigzag (see Stitch Chart, pp.164-165).

4. Turn the seam allowance of the elastic down. Reinforce the seam at the edge with a small bartack. To sew a bartack, set your machine to zigzag with a length of 0 and stitch back and forth several times, securing the seam allowance to the binding.

DECORATIVE ELASTIC

1. This type of elastic is sewn with the right side facing the fabric. If you're sewing to a straight area, install the elastic with excess on either end. For a circle, such as a neckline or armhole, join the elastic in a circle before installing. To do this, overlap the ends of the elastic slightly (about $^3/8"$) and stitch to form a circle.

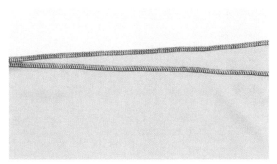

2. Determine if you will finish the edge of your garment. There is no correct answer; it's about what works for your fabric. On a lightweight fabric you may not want the extra bulk of an overlock. If you are using a fabric that is rolling or wants to run when stretched a lot, finishing the edges is a good idea.

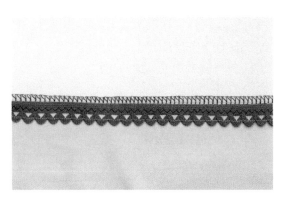

3. With right sides together, place your trim along the edge, aligning the raw edge with the non-decorative edge. Stitch the elastic to the edge using a chainstitch, two row coverstitch, narrow single-step zigzag stitch, or lightning stitch (see Stitch Chart, pp.164-165). Stitch close to the decorative edge of the elastic. If you did not finish your raw edge previously, trim any excess edge that sticks out above the elastic.

4. After it is secure, turn back and topstitch. Use a chainstitch, two row coverstitch, or 3-step zigzag (see Stitch Chart, pp.164-165). If you are using a three-step zigzag, set it to a wide width. You now have a neat and pretty decorative edge.

STRETCH LACE

This type of trim is usually found on spools in the lingerie section of a fabric store. There are so many options: lace with seam allowances that can be sewn into a garment seam, elastics to finish or use as straps, or lovely scalloped lace with variegated width.

Lace trims can be installed just about any way that you see fit. Using a lace trim as a finish can be as simple as overlaying it around your neckline and stitching it down.

One thing I love about lace trims is that you can use the zigzag stitch to install them and the stitch practically disappears into the lace. Even with an arsenal of machines at my disposal, I still do this quite often.

Some elastic laces do not have a seam allowance built into them. Many of these have variegated widths with pretty scalloped edges on both sides. Because there is no seam allowance, these can be sewn in many places, not just in seams.

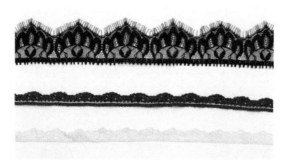

Other elastics are manufactured with a small seam allowance for sewing to your fabric. These are designed to be sewn in a seam, or at a hem or other edge.

CHECK THE STRETCH

Be sure to test your lace for good stretch and recovery. The only real issue I run into with this is due to age of the trim. Sometimes if a trim is old, it will crack or not return when stretched. You should also check the hand feel of the lace and make sure you are okay with how it feels against your skin. Usually they are soft, especially if you found it in the lingerie section. Once or twice, I've accidentally bought a pesky piece of lace that's a little itchy.

STRETCH LACE WITHOUT SEAM ALLOWANCE

When sewing on stretch lace that has no seam allowance, the lace is overlapped onto the fabric and sewn down. You can use a small zigzag stitch for this.

Lace trim overlaying a neckline can be done with a lace that is either a set width, or variegated. This neckline is finished with set width lace trim.

Variegated lace trim can also be set in the same way. Stitch slowly to work around the lace's curves.

INSTALLING A STRETCH LACE EDGE

1. Begin installation with a closed neckline. Pin the lace around the neckline, allowing for a small overlap at the shoulder seam.

2. Check placement; if you are using a wider width lace you can position the lace to show either more skin or more fabric beneath. Don't forget that you may be adding to your garment if the pattern was designed to be hemmed or seamed, so you may also choose to trim the neckline down if your lace is very wide.

3. Overlap the lace at the ends. When using a variegated lace trim, a deep scallop or shape can be tricky to match up at the ends due to the curves. Play with the position of the lace along the neckline until you can get a match.

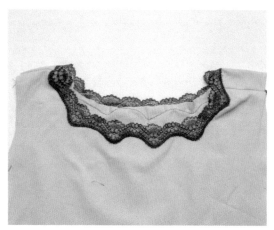

4. Use a small, narrow zigzag to stitch the lower edge of the lace to the garment. Set the length and width of the stitch to 1mm.

5. Overlap the ends of the lace and stitch the overlap down with a zigzag. If your lace is busy, the edge will be unnoticeable.

6. If your lace does not seem busy enough to hide a raw edge with a simple zigzag, you can instead fold each raw edge of lace under $^1/_8$"-$^1/_4$" and stitch it down with a small zigzag.

7. Wide lace sometimes needs two rows of stitching to prevent the lace from flapping around. Start by determining the first place to secure the lace to the neckline, usually around the bottom of the lace. Stitch with a small zigzag.

8. Once secure, assess what parts may need additional security. Pin and then stitch with a narrow zigzag. Pin carefully and stitch slowly to prevent bubbles from forming between the rows of stitching.

PEEK-A-BOO LACE

Lace can also be applied as a decorative band anywhere simply by zigzagging the edges to the garment. If you use a color that is similar to the fabric, you may find that the lace becomes lost. This black lace is a poor read on the black background.

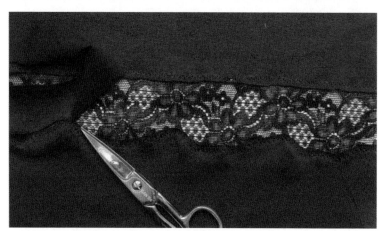

If you want to achieve more of a peek-a-boo look, you can trim away any excess fabric from behind the lace to allow the lace to be more visible. Small scissors work best for this.

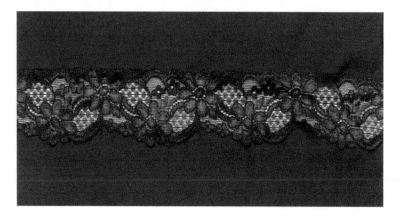

Trimming away the back makes a huge difference to the style. The lace is now much more prominent.

The lace cups on this slip were created from one small piece of variegated stretch lace. The original lace piece had scallops on both sides, and the piece was cut in half lengthwise to create two pieces, each with one scalloped edge.

STRETCH LACE WITH SEAM ALLOWANCE

Lace may also have seam allowances knit into them at one or both edges. For these types, you can sew them on with a clean finish, or applied over a raw edge.

METHOD 1: CLEAN FINISH METHOD

1. For a clean finish, install the lace so that the seam allowance is on the inside of the garment. Pin the lace around the opening, overlapping the ends by $3/8$". Pin right sides together, with raw edge of the fabric aligned with the seam allowance of the lace.

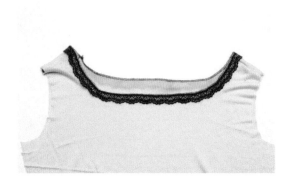

2. Stitch the lace to the opening using a three-thread overlock, mock overlock, 3-step zigzag, or single-step zigzag (see Stitch Chart, pp.164-165).

3. Turn the seam allowance to the inside and topstitch using a chainstitch, very narrow zigzag, or lightening stitch (see Stitch Chart, pp.164-165). Use a small, narrow zigzag to stitch down the $3/8$" lace overlap.

METHOD 2: RAW EDGE METHOD

1. Pin lace over the raw edge on the right side of the garment. For a circular opening, overlap the ends of the lace $^3/_8$".

2. Stitch lace to the fabric along the lace seam allowance using a chainstitch, very narrow zigzag, or lightning stitch (see Stitch Chart, pp.164-165). If necessary, trim excess fabric close to the stitching. Use a narrow zigzag to stitch down the $^3/_8$" lace overlap.

LACE EDGING IN A SEAM

Stretch lace can also be sandwiched between two pieces of fabric when sewing a seam together for a pretty edging. Simply place the lace along the edge between two layers before stitching together.

FACING

Facings are one of the oldest tricks in the book, and probably one you are familiar with if you've sewn with wovens. A facing provides a beauti- ful, clean finish on any edge. But when working with knits, there are a few things to consider.

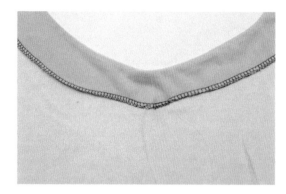

Knits are typically not as rigid as wovens, so if you have a facing at a "V" seam, you may have trouble keeping the facing laying down flat. Sew a small hand tack to keep it in place.

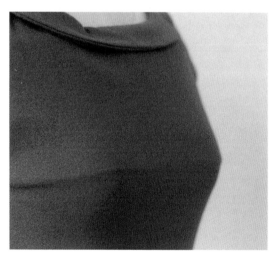

Think about where the facing will lay on the interior of your garment. If it is cutting across mid-bust, you may see a seam underneath due to the stretch. Consider trimming facings so they don't show through on tight areas.

If you do choose to use a facing, invest in some lightweight knit interfacing. Check that it stretch- es. This interfacing is almost always available in the interfacing area of your fabric store and will provide additional stability for your facings.

LINING

For the look of a perfect clean finish, use a lining instead of a facing. I find them less time consuming, and you don't need to worry about interfacing. This is by far my favorite clean finishing method. If you are working with a pattern that does not have a lining already made for the garment, never fear. Drafting your own is a cinch.

1. First trace the pattern pieces you want to line. For this example, I will use the bodice of the Colette Patterns Moneta dress. Trace off your selected pieces.

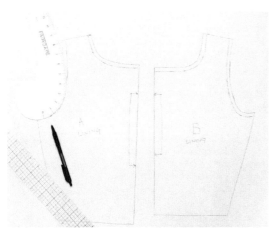

2. Measure and remove $^3/_{16}$" from the outside finished edges of the lining pieces. For this example, it will be from the neckline and armholes. Removing this accounts for the turn of cloth, the way fabric forms around the curves of the seams, and prevents a baggy lining. $^3/_{16}$" is more a bit more than you would remove when working with a woven pattern, but due to the nature of knits, it is good to have a little bit of wiggle room when doing curves and two layers. If you do a contrast lining, you definitely want that lining to stay on the inside of the garment.

3. If you use a different fabric for your lining, make sure that it has the same stretch properties as the main fabric. If not, you may encounter issues when wearing your garment. If the lining has less stretch, it may restrict your garment; If more, it may show in areas you don't want it to, like the neckline.

> **HEMS**

Many home sewists find hems to be a challenge on knit garments, especially those who don't own a serger or a coverstitch. This is where it is time to get creative! We'll take a look at several hems that are done on different machines, but you can also try many of the edge finishes we've discussed on necklines and armholes. Why not finish a hem with an edge of lace (pp.149-155), decorative elastic (p.147), or even a raw edge rolling band (pp.144-145)? The possibilities are endless!

The rolled hem is a narrowly stitched hem made by a serger. It's a fast and easy way to finish light- to medium weight knits. Try adding a pop of color with contrasting thread.

The banded hem can be used to create a variety of looks, from a subtle narrow band to a bold block of color. It can be sewn with or without a serger or coverstitch.

The coverstitch hem is most frequently found on ready-to-wear knit garments. It requires a coverstitch machine.

The twin needle hem imitates the look and functionality of the coverstitch, but it can be sewn with just a standard sewing machine, or combination of standard sewing machine and serger.

ROLLED HEM

The rolled hem is also sometimes called a marrow edge or lettuce edge and is created on a serger. You may use fluff thread or regular sewing thread, depending on the look you are going for.

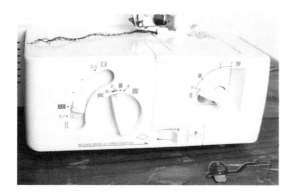

1. To set up your serger, remove the left-hand needle. Remove or disengage the stitch finger on your serger. Lower the stitch width and the stitch length (many sergers have a length and width labeled "R" for rolled hems). Raise your lower looper tension a little and sew test pieces, continuing to adjust the lower looper tension until your stitching is perfect.

2. Stitch the hem of the fabric to create a standard rolled hem. With the shorter width, length, and only one needle, you will have a very neat encased hem.

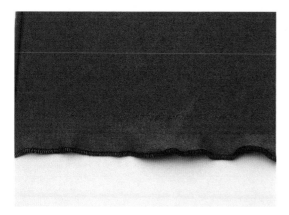

For a rippled lettuce edge, stretch your fabric as you sew. This works best if the area you are sewing is on the crossgrain. Remember to always test sew first to get an idea of how much stretch you need to get the effect you want.

BANDED HEM

Earlier in this chapter (pp.132-134) we talked about doing bands for neck openings and edges with curves, but they can easily be added to sleeves and skirts as hem finishes. This is a great finish for including pattern, color, or just a neat finish without a serger. Bands can be subtle and narrow or dramatic and wide.

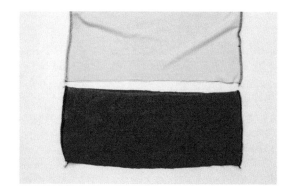

1. Measure the hem and draft band pieces of the same length. Determine how wide you would like the band to be. Add seam allowance to this number. Double this number to get the width of your band. For example, for a finished band of 2" with a $^3/_8$" seam allowance, the band piece should be 4 $^3/_4$". With right sides together, stitch band pieces at the side seams.

2. With wrong sides together, fold band in half lengthwise. With right sides together, line up raw edge with the raw edge of the garment. Stitch in a continuous circle, using the four-thread overlock, mock overlock, single-step zigzag, or three-step zigzag (see Stitch Chart, pp.164-165).

3. Turn seam allowance to the inside. If necessary, steam the garment to finish. This finish can also be perfect for sleeve cuffs and hems, and even works on curved hems.

COVERSTITCH HEM

The coverstitch creates the most common hem you will find on ready to wear. Sewing a hem with the coverstitch is quick, easy, and clean. It also provides a great deal of stretch and durability.

Follow the coverstitch instructions in chapter 5 (see pp.82-83) to learn how to stitch a hem using the coverstitch.

Some machines allow up to 3 needles. With these types of machines, you can create either a two row or three row coverstitch, depending on how many needles you insert (see pp.84-85).

TWIN NEEDLE HEM

If you want to get the look of the coverstitch, you can purchase a twin needle for your home sewing machine. This gives two needle stitch lines on the outside of the garment. For this finish, try using a stabilizing tape to help keep the hem neat (see p.93).

Follow the twin needle hem instructions in Chapter 6 (see pp. 92-93) to learn how to stitch a hem using a twin needle.

Both the front and back of the twin needle hem look very similar to the coverstitch. The main difference is that the coverstitch is designed for knits, so there is less chance of your hem becoming stretched or uneven as you sew.

CHAPTER REVIEW

- Stitching together a knit garment can be accomplished either with or without a serger, but always remember that your stitches must be able to stretch with the garment.

- Clear elastic is useful as both a stabilizer or a functional elastic to create shirring.

- Stabilizing tapes can be used to prevent fabric from getting stretched and wavy when you sew.

- Openings such as necklines and armholes can be finished in a multitude of creative ways, including self fabric bands, self fabric binding, rolling bands, fold over elastic, with decorative elastic, or with stretch lace.

- You can also use familiar methods like facings and linings to finish edges.

- Hems have a lot of style options, including rolled hems, banded hems, coverstitch hems, or twin needle hems. Hems can even be finished using the same methods you can use for other openings, like necklines!

STITCH CHART

STITCH	MACHINE	STITCH WIDTH	STITCH WIDTH	
THREE THREAD ROLLED EDGE	SERGER	LEFT NEEDLE	R (OR WIDTH RECOMMENDED IN YOUR SERGER MANUAL)	_____
THREE THREAD OVERLOCK	SERGER	LEFT NEEDLE	5MM (OR WIDTH RECOMMEND-ED IN YOUR SERGER MANUAL)	_____
NARROW THREE THREAD OVERLOCK	SERGER	RIGHT NEEDLE	3MM (OR WIDTH RECOMMEND-ED IN YOUR SERGER MANUAL)	_____
FOUR THREAD OVERLOCK	SERGER	LEFT NEEDLE, RIGHT NEEDLE	5MM (OR WIDTH RECOMMEND-ED IN YOUR SERGER MANUAL)	_____
FIVE THREAD SAFETY STITCH	SERGER	LEFT NEEDLE, RIGHT NEEDLE	5.6MM (OR WIDTH RECOMMEND-ED IN YOUR SERGER MANUAL)	_____
TWO NEEDLE THREE THREAD COVERSTITCH	COVERSTITCH	LEFT NEEDLE, RIGHT NEEDLE	_____	_____
CHAINSTITCH	COVERSTITCH	ONE OF EITHER LEFT NEEDLE, MIDDLE NEE-DLE, OR RIGHT NEEDLE	_____	_____
THREE NEEDLE FOUR THREAD COVERSTITCH	COVERSTITCH	LEFT NEEDLE, MIDDLE NEEDLE, RIGHT NEEDLE	_____	_____
THREE -STEP ZIGZAG	SEWING MACHINE	SINGLE NEEDLE	1.0-1.5MM	_____
SINGLE-STEP ZIGZAG	SEWING MACHINE	SINGLE NEEDLE	1.5MM	_____
NARROW ZIGZAG	SEWING MACHINE	SINGLE NEEDLE	0.5MM	_____
VERY NARROW ZIGZAG	SEWING MACHINE	SINGLE NEEDLE	0.2MM	_____
MOCK OVERLOCK	SEWING MACHINE	SINGLE NEEDLE	2.0-2.5MM	_____
LIGHTNING STITCH	SEWING MACHINE	SINGLE NEEDLE	2.5MM	_____
STRAIGHT STITCH	SEWING MACHINE	SINGLE NEEDLE	0MM	_____
DECORATIVE STRETCH STITCHES	SEWING MACHINE	SEWING MACHINE	SEE YOUR MANUAL	_____
TWIN NEEDLE HEM	SEWING MACHINE	TWIN NEEDLE (1/4 WIDTH RECOMMENDED FOR HEMMING)	0MM	_____

	STITCH LENGTH	USES	MORE INFORMATION
→	R (OR LENGTH RECOMMENDED IN YOUR SERGER MANUAL)	HEM, EDGE FINISH	P. 64
→	2.5-3.0MM	SOMEWHAT NARROW, NON-BULKY SEAMS FOR AREAS THAT DO NOT HAVE HIGH STRESS. CAN ALSO BE USED AS A FINISH ON KNITS OR WOVENS TO STOP UNRAVELING.	P. 64
→	2.5-3.0MM	VERY NARROW, NON-BULKY SEAMS FOR UNDERWEAR, NECKBANDS, ETC.	P. 64
→	2.5-3.0MM	STRONG SEAMS ON ALL GARMENT TYPES.	P. 65
→	2.5-3.0MM	VERY STRONG SEAMS FOR HEAVY WOVENS, SUCH AS DENIM OR CANVAS.	P. 66
→	2.5-3.0MM	HEM, EDGE FINISH	P. 84
→	2.5MM-3.0MM	EDGESTITCH, TOPSTITCH	P. 84
→	2.5-3.0MM	HEM, EDGE FINISH	P. 85
→	5.0-5.5MM	SEAMS, EDGE FINISH, INSTALLING ELASTIC, EDGESTITCH, TOPSTITCH	P. 89
→	3.0-3.5MM	SEAMS, EDGE FINISH, EDGESTITCH, TOPSTITCH	P. 90
→	2.5MM	NARROW SEAMS, EDGESTITCH, TOPSTITCH	P. 90
→	3.0MM	EDGESTITCH, TOPSTITCH (VERY TIDY, ALMOST STRAIGHT STITCH)	P. 90
→	5.0-5.5MM	SEAMS, EDGE FINISH	P. 90
→	1.0MM	SEAMS, EDGESTITCH, TOPSTITCH	P. 90
→	2.0-3.0MM	SEAMS, EDGESTITCH, TOPSTITCH ONLY ON AREAS THAT REQUIRE LITTLE STRETCH	P. 91
→	SEE YOUR MANUAL	SEAMS, EDGE FINISH, EDGESTITCH, TOPSTITCH, DECORATION	P. 91
→	3.0MM	HEM, EDGE FINISH	P. 92-93

Withdrawn

Made in the USA
Lexington, KY
01 June 2016